THE LOVE THAT ONCE HEALED ME IS THE SAME LOVE THAT DESTROYED ME

UNKNOWN PROPHET

authorHOUSE®

AuthorHouse™
1663 Liberty Drive
Bloomington, IN 47403
www.authorhouse.com
Phone: 1 (800) 839-8640

Published by AuthorHouse   06/05/2017

ISBN: 978-1-5246-9342-8 (sc)
ISBN: 978-1-5246-9343-5 (e)

Print information available on the last page.

King James Version (KJV)
Public Domain

Contents

I Dedicate this Book to:

All Hurting, Hopeless, Unloved,

Battered and Unbelieving People.

To people who need to know that

Jesus is still A Healer, A Deliverer

A Judge, A Doctor and A Lover.

God Has Won Again

A Salvation   Healing

Teaching   Pastor

WHAT INSPIRED ME TO WRITE THIS BOOK?

I WROTE THIS BOOK TO INSPIRE SO MANY PEOPLE WHO IS LOVING ON THE WRONG THING OR THINGS. I HAD LITTLE FAITH WITH LITTLE POWER. WHEN I STARTED BELIEVING EVERY WORD OF GOD, I GOT MORE POWER. I WANT SO MANY PEOPLE TO KNOW ABOUT THE POWER OF GOD. HOW HE HAS NO RESPECT OF PERSON (ANYONE CAN RECEIVE HIS POWER). WHEN GOD BEGAN TO SHOW ME HIS POWER IN MY LIFE I BEGAN TO LISTEN. HE SHOWED ME HOW AND TAUGHT ME HOW TO OVER COME ABUSE, CONTROLLING, NOT BEING LOVED, FEAR AND MOST OF ALL BEING DEFEATED. AM NOT GETTING DEFEATED ANY MORE AND THIS IS WHAT I WANT FOR YOU. THE DEVIL, THE WORLD OR FLESH (MYSELF) CAN'T DEFEAT ME. I WANT TO HELP YOU (IN OTHER WORDS) TO STOP YOU FROM CONTINUING HURTING LIKE I DID. MAKING WRONG DECISIONS AND NOT ACCEPTING REJECTION. I WOULD LIKE FOR YOU TO READ THIS BOOK AND APPLY IT TO YOUR LIFE OR SOMEONE ELSE LIFE. LETTING YOU OR THEM KNOW ABOUT THE POWER OF GOD. I GIVE TO YOU WHAT GOD GAVE TO ME. HIS WORD OF FREEDOM. ALL I DID WAS BELIEVED AND LEARNED OF HIM. MY TESTIMONIES THAT GOD HAS MADE AVAILABLE WILL TEACH YOU ABOUT JUST BELIEVING.

PS. GOD HAS ALL POWER; IF YOU JUST BELIEVE IT.

This is Pastor Elect Lady sold out Soldier for Jesus Christ.

I would like to share some testimonies of my
life that Jesus has made available.
It is so good to testify of
what God has done in your life.

By letting others know that God has no respect of person
(Romans 2:11). He will do the same for you or someone
you might know that needs His Power also.

CHAPTER 1

Beginning of Life

My life as a child was a very hard life. By this I mean I had a place to live, lots of food to eat, clothes to wear but didn't have motherly love. I would see my Mother love my Sister and Brothers but not me. Well hold on to that thought until I get to that part. We think that because hardship comes in our lives at an early age, somebody sinned (John 9:2-3). Well no one cause this.

Some of these testimonies where before I came to God or before I came all the way; sold out for Jesus. At a very early age; I was a black stallion horse (meaning, I didn't won't anything or anybody to ride upon me). I didn't want anything good to ride on me. I didn't have love so I couldn't love myself. But I tried to love others. I didn't trust anyone rather they were of God or not. Nothing good I would let in, only dark and cold things would I let ride on and in me. Didn't want others to hurt like I was hurted? Love children, seniors and animals. Why? Because they are helpless and sometimes people didn't loved them or stop loving them. I am letting you in a little about me. Remember having ¼ of my index finger on my left hand cut off. I lived in the Desire Projects in the 50's and medicine wasn't as powerful as it is today. I was unable as I was told to get my finger sewed on. The devil wanted me at a very early age but he couldn't have me. I was told that I was shooting sugar water out of my bottle at a neighbor throw the cracks of the front iron steel door and the neighbor shut the door tight. Well in those days you had to shut the doors hard, well he did.

I was only three (3) years old and was told I had just made it. They said I stop talking for a long time. I don't remember the pain but I have

1

the evidence of ¼ of my finger gone. God blessed me as I was told about what happen to my finger. This was my second miracle God did in my life.

The first miracle was when he gave me life. Now in this Project (Desire) My Mother, I, my sister and brothers lived with my aunt in a four bedroom apartment. There were a lot of people who lived in this apartment. My aunt, her husband and seven (7) children. My mother and three of us, my other aunt had three (3) children also. The three other Aunts who had no children and our Grandmother. She was our backbone of the family and we lived together. Now no one could tell we all lived there because we had lots of food, clean clothes to wear and pallets to lay on. We would get our baths and run to lay on the pallets (only one or two bedspreads and a sheet for covering). We could watch television and went to sleep on our pallets. We knew what a bed look like but we also knew those pallets were our beds. I was just one of the children that weren't like very much. My aunts and cousins, even my brothers and sister didn't like me. Maybe because my mother didn't love me. I mean; the kind of love that is showed to your child. Everyone except my Grandmother treated me different from the other children. I just knew my mother had my older brother who felled off the Project stairs on some bricks and became cripple. I heard my Father asked her to move with him to Texas. She told him no after she found out another lady was pregnant for him again with a second child. This was told to me by My Grandmother and I believed it. Maybe I came at the wrong time in her life. Maybe the hurt my Father put on her; she probably didn't know she was putting it on me.

CHAPTER 2

———————◉———————

Breath Taken Away

Now let's talk about the time my life was taken away from me. I was talking to a friend that lies about a lot of things. She began to tell me about her niece who was taken in the weeds or miniature jungle. She began to say how the man that took her then let her go after seven hours and never touch the little girl. They prayed for hours and God answered their prayers. I said to her I don't believe you because you lie so much. I was saved but not submissive all the way to The Holy Ghost. I heard The Holy Ghost say to me; you should remember. Now do you remember when I kept you? Then I began to cry (because I wasn't allowed to remember this). God had taken it away from me.

The day my life was taken away. Now I remember when I was eight years old, when I heard the Voice of Power. It sounded like a man unknown. I hear this same voice every day now and it's Jesus. If you don't believe this just continue reading about The Glory of God in my life. While living in the Desire Projects, we lived across the street from the weeds or miniature jungle on Alvar Street. Everything I believe was in this jungle, except Lions, Tigers and Bears. Every year during the summer time, blackberries and red berries would grow on the trees. Me, my brother and two cousins went to pick berries. While we were picking berries we heard something running through the weeds (jungle). It sounded like it was running faster than we could believe. Then the running stopped. At this time we looked around to see if we could see what or who was running so fast. We didn't see anything or anybody. So we started climbing higher in the trees because the berries looked so good at the top.

Then my life was taken away from me. As I am writing this I began to cry. Please Parents Love and Keep Your Eyes on Your Children, and Always Share Your Life with Them. They are just smaller, but are equipped with the same senses you have. They hurt, they laugh, they remember, they don't forget or even forgive. They need love in order to give love. Could you just remember that they are just like us; just smaller?

A man heavily built-dark brown in color, strong smelling grab me out of the tree where I was picking berries. He throws me over his shoulders and began to run with me in the weeds (jungle). He was running so fast with me on his shoulders, as I was screaming **No, No.** I was so afraid when he took me. He took the breath out of me. I guess my brother and my two cousins began to run across the street where we lived at in the Projects to call my mother or whomever they could find to help me. I remember being on this man shoulders that smelled like death (sour). You know some people say death smells like something you never smelled before (very bad). He brought me through the jungle running so fast with me.

That's when war became real. He put my head on a large piece of wood or log, and put a knife between my neck and left jaw bone and said don't say a word. He began to say I will kill you; if you move or say something. So I didn't say anything to him. Until now at the age of 61 year old I can still recognize him. He began to pull down my pants and panties and ask me how old are you. I think I said eight years old or something. All I know I was not develop like a young lady yet. He continues pulling my pants and panties down further and I went into shock. I had never seen a man private parts before and especially not one that look like it was dripping with water (bad water). It was so fat and had such a bad odor. Jesus please help me. Just taking a break-Crying-Crying-Yes Crying. God is so good to me. He was beginning to open my legs wider and wider. My Mother never told me about God (Jesus). I don't remember going to church; I don't remember even hearing her or my family talk about church or God (Jesus) before. I don't know what to say or do. I remember somebody one day was talking about God and said that he lives in the sky. So I begin to look up in the sky because I heard he lives there. They said he was Great and Powerful. Somebody said in a conversation; if you call on God he will come and help you. I am only eight years old. I begin to say, God help me please. Please God help me to myself. I laid down there with my pants and panties at my knees. So I look in the sky again and began to say over and over God help me please. God help me.

Then The War Began:

I heard that man say be quiet. As he was opening my legs wider I began to cry harder. He was coming closer to me to put his private part inside of me. I heard the noise of many people running in the weeds (jungle) toward us. A strong voice said; leave my child alone. Then the noise of many men running toward us stopped. The weeds were still moving strong. The Voice said to the man the Second Time (The First Time the man looked around and saw no one). Then he continued making me open my legs wider and keep them that way. Then the Second Voice Sounded Even Stronger than the First Voice. As he was trying to put his private part inside of me. The Voice said; leave my Heavenly Child alone. It had so much power, that the man couldn't put his private part in me. He looked around and begin to run toward the back of the weeds (jungle) shaking with fear uncontrollable. I still was looking at the sky calling on God. Then I could hear my Mother voice running through the weeds (jungle) calling my name. Where she was; I think it was yet so far away from me. Now I can't remember until this day. Who or how I got off the ground and who pulled my clothes up. Who directed me towards My Mother voice and others voices that was calling my name. As I was walking towards the sound of their voices, the weeds was opening up for me. So I finally met My Mother and her friends. After 50 years passed by; I forgot about this Miracle God performed in my life. I was told that I stopped talking for two years. So when The Holy Ghost brought it back to my remembrance; I asked my mother about this. I asked her did she hear a voice in the weeds (jungle) and were the weeds opening up for you giving you a way to me (Psalm 121: 5-8). The Lord kept me and is still keeping me. If you can just let God keep you. Now I guess you say how Pastor? (Have faith in who he is) (Hebrews 11:6). My Mother said; yes the weeds were opening up and she heard a Voice Powerful say leave My Heavenly Child alone. Now until this day; GOD calls me HEAVENLY CHILD.

CHAPTER 3

For Being Who You Are

I was a smart little girl in math, science and lots of other subjects. I couldn't read because my family were Creoles, and some of us spoke broken language. I was one of them that got it from generations before me and others. The broken language causes you to say and spell what you heard; that's bad. If you were trying to go to an Ivory School (99% free from fighting and teaching you how to become a lady) you want to beable to speak correctly. Just image if I or you or us was that other 1% of mixer. Not all the family spoke bad but I did. My Mother never helped me with my homework because I showed her my good grades. I just wanted her to give me some attention but she gave it to my brothers and sister. My older brother was cripple from a baby from a fall. My little brother was her heart (until this day). My sister had a lung disease. Just wanted a little attention. Now I understand as an adult how she loved me, but never had time to show me or tell me this. My brothers and sister came first because of their sickness. She never hugged or kissed me for being her child or for doing a great job. I learned how can someone love you; if they don't know how to love. I didn't know that then.

I went to Saint Phillip the Apostle Catholic School. By going there I went to church all the time and learned about the Love of God. I wanted to be a Nun because of the love I felt in God. I went to Saint Phillip from the sixth grade until the eighth grade. The kids (not all) who live in the Projects (Oh by the way My Mother got her own apartment in the Desire) like to fight a lot. The kids wanted to fight me because my mother had a color television set. I was light skinned and wear nice clean clothes; believe it or not. Never knew why I was fighting. They fought me from the sixth grade until the eighth grade until I graduated. Then I stop getting beat up and I became the winner in every fight after that. They taught me how to fight after getting beat up so much. I learned how to hit them where it hurt. I Hate, I hated to fight because it always hurt rather you win or lose. I wasn't a scary person just one who needed help. I didn't want to tell my mother. My Mother was ignorant; she curses so much. I didn't want the kids to tease me and laugh at me. It would have cause me to get beat up more. Her name was Ms. B. and she would listen to her brother, sisters and friends. They tell her to punch me in my face and have me to run home crying. I didn't fight back because her brother and sisters would beat me too. I saw her and said; this is really you. The one who use to beat me up with your brother and sisters. Now please do it now. She must have seen the Spirit of Revenge on my face. She was so Fearful (that bad grass). Ms. B didn't say a word. She looked at me with her mouth open. I just wanted her to experience Fear as I did as a young girl. I felt it was right to do. I remember when I was a girl eleven years old and how I hurtled. This was not right and God handled me for this. I had to repent to God First. Now when I see Ms. B I will repent to her and tell her about the God I serve. I pray that God would let me see her again in Jesus name (Romans 12:18-19).

Now at Saint Philip the Apostle School I was smart in everything but reading. The kids would make fun of me when I read. Well this one girl who name is Ms. SH would really make fun of me. It's time to graduate from the eighth grade to senior high school. The ones that use to beat me up went to a Public School. I wanted to go to one of the best High Schools in the world. It was Saint Mary's Academy for girls. You see; I heard about this school and wanted to go there badly. The kids not all who teased me about I couldn't read wanted to go there. Now Ms. SH was so horrible with teasing me about going to Saint Mary's. She said that they will not accept me because I couldn't read well. In order to get in Saint Mary's you had to take a placement test. Ms. SH, I and five other girls were going to take the placement test. Every day at school (Oh – yes she was in my eighth grade class at Saint Philip) she would tell me how stupid and dumb I was because I didn't read well. I knew this was not true. I learned that God (Jesus) from this school Saint Philip enough to call on his help.

So it was Do or Die Testing Day. Pass the test or get killed or kill myself. If I had went to a Public School I would fight a lot. Finally the test day came and it was the Beginning of New Life, New Environment and New Friends for me if; I get accepted. This was what I believed in and what I ask God for. We had to wait two weeks before we would know if we passed or not. The Nuns came to our class room from Saint Mary's Academy to tell us who passed. Who need to go Summer School for Math or Reading or both? They also came to say who failed the test. The Nuns begin to talk to us who had taken the placement test about the school. Then they begin to call our names in order. Three girls passed without Summer School and two of you have to go to Summer School and one failed in everything. Ms. SH looked at me like she knew I was the one that failed. She was laughing in my face but I believed what I was taught. I was taught how and who God Helps. I had asked God to give me a New Environment. I was feeling hopeless at this time. Now names were called and you know Ms. SH still was making me feel bad. My name came before hers and the other girls name came before mines. Now the other four girls were accepted. It's between me and Ms. SH. One of us has to go to summer school and one of us failed. When they called my name I had made up in my mind to just Die or Kill myself. The Nun said Linda, I said; Yes Sister and she said you have been accepted. You have to go summer school for reading. I began to look up in the class ceiling Thanking God. Tears running down my eyes. I knew God was real and he loved me. So much just to give me a chance to have a New Environment, Friends and a Whole New Life. It was Ms. SH turn. The Nun told her they were sorry but she was not accepted. She began to tell the Nuns that Linda and I last names are almost the same (M c). She began to say to the Nuns that they made a mistake between us two. The Nuns said no we didn't; Linda passed every part of the placement test accept the reading part. They told her she didn't score higher enough to be accepted. Now did I laugh at her (NO)? I felt so bad for her because I knew if it was me I would be hurting like her. You see; God gave me favor over the enemy (Matthews 5:44). The laughing stopped and Ms. SH told me how sorry she was for teasing me. How she would not do that to no one else. I went to Saint Mary's summer school for reading and passed.

At Saint Marys' I was placed in a class (9-4) nine four meaning; I was in the ninth grade but in the D class. The lowest class you can be in the (9ᵗʰ) ninth grade. I didn't care at first, just so glad to be there. I had a History Teacher who was a Nun. She would call on me a lot to read. She and the class not all of them would make fun of me. One day I answer her back in anger. She sent me to the office to be punished. I was so hurt at that time I didn't care. So I was given the paddle. By the way I worked after school for part of my tuition because it was too much for my mother to pay. You see; my mothers' heart was softened by God to let me go to this expensive school. I could remember when I got the paddle for answering back.

She would put the School Loud Speakers on so the Whole School could hear her beat me and me crying. I had a choice to get the paddle over the Loud Speakers or call my mother to school for this. I didn't want my mother to come to school for me. My mother would have made it worst for me. I didn't care if the children heard me. I had a New Life there and I had to adjust to their rules. I was just Thanking God for Loving Me. So after the beating I had to go to work. The Nun that was over the work crew was Sis. Joseph. A lot of the students thought she was a mean Nun, well I didn't know. I would just do my work and she would check it and let me go home. So I was late the day I got beat at the office. Sis Joseph asked me what happen. She said she didn't like what was done to me. I begin to tell her how my History Nun Teacher would make fun of me with the kids about my reading. I begin to cry to her and told her how I always had trouble reading. She said to me, do you want to learn how to Read and I said; Yes Sister. She said you must come every day after you have done your work and stay longer after school so I can help you. She said it just the background that you have. Creoles have a problem reading and pronouncing words correctly. I would stay after school for hours every day. I did that for almost a year then school ended. My grades had picked up and I could read on my class level. The next year came for school and placement. I was moved from (9/4) which is still the D class to the (10/2) which is the tenth grade and the B class. Meaning; above avenge class. I want you to know what the Devil meant for evil, God makes for good. I graduated from the B class with five awards. I had the highest score in Math. I had the highest award in Home Economies. I received the Crisco award with a scholar ship in Economies. To God Be The Glory. What I asked God for as a teenager he gave it to me. At this time I knew God a little more and enough to believe in him. Why; I Just Believed (James 1:5-6)?

CHAPTER 4

Knowledge of God

I remember at the age of fifteen I met my first boyfriend Mr. X. I met him at one of Saint Mary's dances. He said to me that he was going to marry me because I was just like his mother (Now remember that). I laughed at him but it came to pass. I let Mr. X come to visit me at my mother's house with her permission. My Mother cursed so much that I was becoming what she called me. I wanted so bad to come from under this abuse. I got pregnant for someone **I didn't know or loved.** I told my friend that I was pregnant because I knew her mother had given her an abortion. She told her Mother who was My Mother's friend. In the seventy's abortion was done by Mid-Wives which was cheaper. They weren't Doctors or Nurses just Vow Doo Workers I called them. I had to go to the Vow Doo Workers because I was going to college. My mother didn't want to be embarrass because of the mistake I made (it wasn't a mistake just a bad choice I made). I went to the Vow Doo Lady. I remember she put a piece of iron in me. (That's what it felt like). I thought not just the baby would die but me too. I guess I had to make a choice but my thoughts were over power with Fear. I bleed a lot but God healed me. He forgave me and stilled loved me. **I asked God to help me and keep me. I told God how sorry I truly was (1 John 1:9).**

He is a Faithful God.

The Old Abuse was temporally gone and the New Abuse comes in. I got married at the age of nineteen to my first boyfriend of four years. Was married to him for twenty four years. Who was taught through his family relationship how to be a Controller? Well at first I didn't think it was all that bad. He did tell me he loved me. His love cost so much that I didn't want it any more. His Father controlled his Mother and him but not the Sister. While being married to Mr. X he was on drugs. He would sleep with my so call friends; batter me and didn't support his family. I was a strong and smart woman. I met an old white lady who liked me a lot. She taught me how to sell houses under her and how to manager apartments. I would sell houses to my friends and she would keep the money for me. I wanted to buy a house for me and my girls. She held my money until I founded a house. I couldn't buy the house by myself. Mr. X was on drugs so bad that he looked like it. His father owned a lot of property and knew the bankers. I ask him to get the house in his name and I will pay for it. He agreed because the agreement was if I didn't pay for it he could have it. His father said he didn't want those white people to see his son looking like that (Broom Stick). Me, his father and mother went to the act of sale and got the house through the Spirit of God. We lived in that house for nineteen years or more. The bank held the first mortgage; his daddy the second and I held the third through The Spirit of God.

Mr. X was a Muslin who would bring us to the temple. We would go to the talk shows and I would sit in the back with the mothers. There were Mothers who had one baby in the stomach and two or more in diapers. While not all husband would have other women or families. I couldn't understand how women were being controlled but I learned. He would come from the Muslin Temple and then fight me. Now did I fight back; yes but after a while you just stop fighting. The drugs, women, money and abuse were getting really bad. I couldn't go to my mother because she would say you made that bed now lay in it. I guess she meant; you made that choice to leave me and marry him. That choice controlled and destroyed me. Please ask God even if you don't know him but wants to know him to help you in making choices. Choices and decisions need to be cover by the Blood and Spirit of God. His mother was one of the sweetness women in the world. She was very Passat and Fearful of her husband. I would ask her how she took those things off her husband. She would say its okay. She was a home body but sweet. She became the mother I never had and my best friend. I couldn't understand Mr. X when he said you are like my mother I didn't understand then but I understand now. I would tell her what he would do me and she would replied a man don't change until he get into his forties. I believed that for a long time (That's Not True Please; Trust Me on this). So when the house note was due and I was short; she would help me. When I got my food stamps, she would give me a dollar for a dollar. This would pay my light bill, etc. She would use her money her husband gave to her to spend on herself and help me sometimes. Every now and then when I would lose the money gambling I blame that on something. I use to say I am depress and that's why I gamble (It was my flesh that wanted it; just another excuse) (Matthews 26:41). I had a Grandmother who loved me and she helped me a lot. She died and my mother-law became my friend. I never remember my mother-law going to church but I knew and believed she knew Jesus. At times when Mr. X would hurt me; she would say call on Jesus three times and he will answer you and help you. So I use to call Jesus name three times when I was hurting and it worked. When Mr. X would come home with passion marks on his neck; I used her method about Jesus. I stop going to the Muslin Temple not because of the Muslin but because he showed me that the religion he was in; was not helping him. He would go to the Temple and then beat me weak. We had three Daughters and as they got older they treated me like their father. I never beat my girls because if I did I would continue beating them to death. Remembering how I was always beaten (Verbal, Physical and Mental). I would give them all the pain my mother and their father gave me. I married him to get away from Abuse of my mother and he became the Greater Abuser than my Mother. I thought I came out Abuse; I made a bad choice. You see ; Mr. X knew the Abuse I was getting and he knew my weakness. He knew I just wanted to be love. I could remember how happy I was when I married Mr. X and in three months the marriage changed. I was under Powerful Controlling Spirits. These Spirits came from my mother-in-law teaching me how to accept the Abuse from Mr. X and my three daughters. It was so bad that I became weak to Controlling and Fear.

Now Let's Talk About Abuse; the Abuser and Jesus. I hope through The Grace of God that you read this. Listen to the Holy Ghost and teach this to others. Why Pastor? Because you love them that much to let them get set free (Matthew 10: 8).

So I had a friend Ms. J who would come to me for worldly advice about her man. The things I would tell her to say and do came to pass. It worked and she won him. I couldn't help myself. I had worldly knowledge which was nothing compared to God's knowledge. I didn't know Ms. J would see how much I was hurting. She would ask me to go to church every Sunday. I would say no each time. I didn't want to serve her God. Why? Because I thought her God should help her and not me. I would say to myself; if she serve such a Perfect God; why she lived the way she was living. I was judging out of ignorance. Not knowing this Wonderful, Loving, Kind, and Powerful God that I now know. Ms. J kept asking me to go to church and I still would answer; no girl. I would just stay home, smoking cigarettes one after another, drinking diet cokes and crying with pain. Playing worldly music that would make me pain more (Love Songs). Talking to my mother-in-law; who would convince me that if Mr. X wanted anyone else he would move with them? He would not come home. Well those statements became my every day words and not the Word of God. Because I didn't know God (Jesus). I just remember what his Mother taught me about Jesus (call on his name three times and he will help you). I had it so bad with his Controlling and her Sighting Skills, until I became like his mother. (He told me I was like his mother when I first met him, now I understand his words he spoke to me). I would get palpitation a sickness of being misuse and I would be unable to speak and worry like she would. I know this had to stop (Him and Her). Now when Mr. X would steal her ring and other things she would call me crying saying what I need to tell him. You see; she knew her controlling, fear possessed husband would not allow him to stay at their house. He was on drugs and he didn't play that. My Mother-in-law taught me how to keep him, how to love him, and how to ignore the abuse. My girlfriend Ms. J would come around me more and more because at that time she and my mother-in-law were my only friends. My Daughter had a baby shower at my house and my Husband; her Father never showed up. He did show up three days later. I lost twenty-five pounds in three days. He had passion marks on his neck and told me, he didn't want me anymore. I never wanted him but I ran from Abuse to Abuse. I had gotten caught up and I was very weak. He came home ; took a bath, change clothes and left again. It was about 1 am in the morning when I called my Mother-in-law, my friend, my all in all. I began to ask her can

I talk to you as a friend and not as a mother-in-law. She said yes; then I began to tell her I was hurting. I did everything you taught me, and what you told me to say. My mother-in-law said to me that one day Mr. X is not going to be able to open your heart up. No matter what he does or say. I ask her about; how her daughter would get a man so quick after breaking up with one. She replied, well my daughter just go and fined her a man. Then it came to my mind that's what I going to do. Find me a man at Lucky Bar. I had made my mind up to sleep with the man I find at Lucky Bar and then kill myself. I went to kill myself. First I got off the phone with my mother-in-law and began to get dressed. I put on my daughter clothes because I had lost so much weight and I wanted something very tight and sexy looking to men. I got dressed; got in my car and had a made up mind about what I planned to do. Had a readymade mind to sleep with a man and then kill myself. I started driving to Lucky Bar. On my way to Lucky Bar; I heard a Voice Speak to me. Well I didn't think anything about it. I had been crying so long, so long I just wanted to die. Then I heard a Voice Speak saying you are just Lonely but you are not Alone because I am with you. I slowed the car down and pulled the car to my left side instead the right side of me. Why? Hang on! So I turned around in the car thinking somebody was in the car; well no one was. I heard that same Voice that said; turn this car around and go back home you are just Lonely but you not Alone. I looked around in the back of the car and no one was there. Then I checked the radio but it was not on. I turned the radio on to see if it works and it did. So I cut the radio off and said out aloud; **Who IsThis? Who Are You?** He (The Voice) said nothing. So now I am passing up an eating place call We Never Close Sandwich Shop. As I was passing this place up there is a turning lane on my left side. I got to the intercession where I could turn if I wanted to. My mind was on what I had planned to do. The Devil was convincing me to drive faster. Well at this point My Car Began to Turn It Self Around. The Car was turning – going toward We Never Close Sandwich Shop. Then I began to say; WHO IS THIS and He said this is me. This is Me JESUS; My Heavenly Child. You just Lonely but you are not Alone, because I am with you. So he (Jesus) began to tell me to go home to talk with him. I was Fearful but also just happy because when Jesus talked to me I felt like a different person. I had Peace, Strength and I wanted to talk to a New Friend. I said to Jesus; let me stop at We Never Close Sandwich Shop. He (Jesus) knew what I was going to do. I felt a high and I needed cigarettes and a large diet coke. I got out the car at We Never Close Sandwich Shop. The shop was full with customers. I went to the registry to ask for change to get cigarettes (We are talking about in the 90's). I order a large diet coke and change. The lady never looked up at me. When the lady went to give me my diet coke and change for cigarettes she looked up at me. She looked again at me and began to scream in a loud voice. Her co-workers came running to the front at the registry where she and I was. Then the customers that were in there (a lot of people on Friday night) came to the registry too. The lady that was waiting on me said to her co-workers and the customers that were in the Sandwich Shop to look at her face (talking about my face). They all were looking at me and I was so hurted I just cried. The lady said to the people look at the light that shines on her face. She said; like God has touched her (Well he did). I went home and talked with Jesus. Jesus saved my life and I surrender my life to him. I stop Cursing, Crying and Hurting. I finally felt Love. Jesus knew I was going to have sex with any man and then kill myself. God loves us so much that he knows what hurts us, who hurt us and what we need to do about it. Thank you Jesus for Loving me. I called Ms. J the next day and ask her to come and get me for church. She never gave up asking me to go to church (Matthew 5:41). We went to church and they were doing an altar call. They said; if you need the Power of The Holy Ghost with the evidence of speaking in tongues come up. I went up and I went out on the floor when Pastor G touched me. Came up with divers of tongues. Speaking different kinds of tongues. Pastor G said God blessed you. I heard that the Holy Spirit with speaking in tongues is keeping Powers. Well I heard through the Grape Vine of Jesus; if you give God your mind, heart and soul you will have these Powers too. That's Powerful-Keeping Power. Try it; you might just like it.

CHAPTER 5

Power of God Inside

I was waiting for the Devil to attack me. So I can speak, and show him the Power that God has given me. I went from killing myself to killing them that wanted to kill me; with the Power of God. I got home from church Mr. X had finally come home and he could see something had taken place in my life. I wasn't crying, fussing or asking him where he had been. I really didn't care. The Spirit of Controlling was broken. The Spirit of Fear didn't live in my mind, heart or soul anymore. Just the love, peace and joy of God begin to live in my mind, heart and soul (2Corinthians 2:17). Now I began to serve God. You see; my God ; Jesus Christ was a Greater and Powerful God than his god Muhammad (a dead god) but my God lives (Matthew 22:32). Mr. X was so mad and hateful toward me. He would say things like, if you don't stop serving this man, who is a prophet (Jesus) I will divorce you.

ABUSE is a spirit that always comes with his cousins; the spirits of pity, low esteem, unloved, hopeless, pleasing, unstable, unwanted and the greatest of all; the spirit of fear (2 timothy 1:7). Well all those spirits lived inside of me. The Abuser, Mr. X knew this and he played mind games with me. I was so use of being abused that I would just let things go. Jesus set me free and I thought being extra kind to his flesh was godly (Well it wasn't). One day I was washing clothes in the garage when he came home loaded. He was so mad because he had a fuss with his father. His father didn't care for him much. He was his mother favorite. When I came out the garage he was waiting on me to hit me (just because). I remember I put my index finger and the one next to it together. My thumb in a circle and said; in the name of Jesus; I said it again in the name of Jesus; I dare you to hit me anymore. I looked him in his eyes without Fear, without feeling Powerless, Hopeless or just Afraid. I said over and over I dare you to hit me in the name of Jesus. It seems like my right hand held that position for a long time. He said to me girl you are crazy talking about this Jesus as if he was God. He said Jesus is just a Prophet not God. He said I am not going to do you nothing. Well I knew Jesus was God and God was Jesus. I knew this not because someone told me that. Not because I had just read about him but because if anyone could stop him from hitting me it would have to be God (Jesus Christ). The one I gave my life to and the one I ask to be my Lord and Savior. The one that I gave my heart, mind and soul to. The one I believe that has all the power. So from that day; Jesus became my Lover, Doctor and Lawyer. The God that made me smile and not frown or look sad. The God that don't let me feel hurt anymore from him at all. So I started being convinced, converted and committed to God. This is what we all need to consider in our life. I call it, the (3) Three C'S for Christ (Matthew 5:4 and Matthew 5:6). You know he was very mad he could not treat me any kind of way. When he would try; I would call on the name of Jesus. Let me tell you what I Heard through the Grape Vine (James 4:7). If We Submit Ourselves To God, Resist The Devil, and He Will Flee From You (James 2:19). At this time the Devil, Mr. X, Flesh and the World were against me. His Mother was told by her son about me serving God (Jesus). She knew that my eyes and heart would be open real soon. What she didn't know when I gave my life to Jesus my eyes came open. My heart was receiving the present of God. His Mother decided to send him to Rehabilitation Center for drugs. We go there for help. I say we go, because my Mother-in-law again believed that this would help our marriage. I still was learning a little more about the Love of God. Mr. X didn't want me to read about Jesus. He would come home with books (cost a lot of money) to challenge certain stories in the Bible. Today I use those books with the help of the Holy Ghost to teach and to set God's people free (when he left me he left those books). We go to the first meeting to get admitted. Then the counselor suggested that I go to a support group meeting for families of addictions. All I got from the meetings is that I was addicted to Mr. X addiction. I knew the 12steps program couldn't help him or help me. I had an addiction that only Jesus could break. I stop going to the meetings and stayed home. I believe until this day he went into the hospital because I was going to leave him and his addiction. I had been learning more and more about Jesus. I would get up in the Morning and Glorify God First. I use to say Good Morning Mr. X but I started saying when I get up---**Good Morning God, Good Morning Jesus, and Good Morning Holy Ghost.** They are the Ones that could make and did make my Mornings Good. When he relies it was over for him. He wanted to divorce me. The reason he gave was that we are serving two different Gods'. He served Muhammad who was and still is a dead god and prophet and I serve Jesus, the Only True and Living God. He began to tell me that Jesus was just a prophet and there was no begotten Son of God. He began to tell me to choose the one I will serve. He said if you choose Muhammad, you would be a great woman. Guess what? Every day he would torment me about Jesus. One day I didn't know God knew what was in my heart and mind. I was cleaning my bathtub out when I heard a voice say-**Whom Would You Forsakes for Me** (Joshua 24:15/24:20) (PROVERBS 9:6) I replied no one Jesus, no one. Mr. X was very anger, mean, hot and wanting to hit me. He couldn't because it seems like when I would put my fingers up and say in the name of Jesus he would not hit me. I said these words with power from on high (you're not going to hit me). I will kill you; I am not afraid of you no more (just don't use the words I will kill you please). His uncle taught him how to get property without my name on it and still be marry to me. He had to apply for a divorce and then he would be able to get the property without my name on it. Mr. X had divorce paper brought to our home where we both lived at. The door bell rung and I answered the door. A Sheriff was at the door. The Sheriff said; is you Linda and I replied; yes. He said you are being served divorce papers. I was in an unbelievable state of mind. I said to him; who sent them? He said just sign here. I look at those divorce papers and my new life in the flesh became real. He thought because I chose to serve Jesus Christ, My God, My Lord, My Savior and My Everything and not his god he didn't come home.

I began to look for a job. God showed me one in the newspaper. I called the ad and they told me to come in. Now it's about 11:45 in the morning. I put my clothes on in about 10 minutes and left the house. The job was about 30 to 40 minutes away from my house. I got to the place from the address I had and it was close. There was a sign that said not in business any more. So the first thing I thought was that I didn't hear from God. I had heard from the Devil and followed him. I cried all the way home. It seem like it took longer to get there and shorter to get home. I left my house at 12 noon and got back home at 12:25 or 12:28pm. I remember looking at my watch because I needed to get my grandson from school. I couldn't go there before 1pm and no later than 5:30pm. I open my living room door and I felt lightness. I went to the garage and open the door and all his painting equipment was gone (ladders and etc.). Then I went to my neighbor house and began to ask her did someone come to my house. She replied that your Husband (Mr. X) came (5) five minutes after you left. He had a truck and (3) three more men with him. She said they began to take something's out the garage and out the house. They just left she said; did you not see them. I lived on a street that went around and instead of going out the way you came in you can go the other way out. I said Thank You Lord. I didn't know why I was crying. I continue crying; for I knew not why. I started walking in my room and saw his clothes gone. He left powerful books that he used to come against me and my Jesus. I now use them for reference about Jesus (now look at Jesus). He left some pictures of Muhammad that I threw away because I didn't want his Spirit around me. I Got on my knees and said Thank You Jesus for loving me. You see; God not the Devil took me on that ride. God did that so we couldn't fight. Mr. X and those men couldn't see me cry. They couldn't see me in a fleshly state of mind; instead of the mind of Christ. They were Muslim too and I told them and showed them about the God I serve (Jesus). I said to myself thank you Jesus (1Corinthains 2:11 / 2:16). I now know why I was crying so much because I had been praying for peace. God gave me peace in everything, every place and with everybody. Now I understand he had to leave because the divorce was coming up and I had received the peace of God in my home.

CHAPTER 6

Being Honor as a Woman of God

I went to a Lawyer who was a friend to both of us and he rejected me. The first time I went to court it was just Jesus and me.

Guess who I saw at court? A man of God who I thought was so powerful in the Word of God. Now just listen so you want be fooled. Look like this man of God saw a ghost. I was his babe in Christ and he was teaching me. Before going to count I asked the church to pray for me. This man of God allowed them to pray for me. He spoke a word to my spirit. He said Sis. Linda your husband needs to give you everything because of the children. He needs to pay wife support and child support. He said your husband should want to take care of you and the children after 24 years of marriage. Just so happen; me and that man of God was going inside the same court room speaking to the same Judge.

The best part about it was what God wanted to show me. Have Faith in me not Man said God. He went first and the Judge said you going to jail if you don't catch up and pay your wife support and child support. He had to leave the Family home. He didn't want to get out their home for the children because he was so mad with his wife. He was caught having a minor girl in their home. His wife was so hurt; she wanted a divorce and to leave him alone forever. This man of God would teach us how we must obey the Law of the land. He was the same Monster my Husband was. God would let you see, hear and be taught about who's real and who's not. I didn't feel bad that I was under his ministry; just felt badly for him. He wasn't living the Word of God he was preaching. I began to look at him under the guides of Christ. (What do you mean Pastor?). As long as he was in the present of God on the pool pit; I honored him. If we went to different functions I didn't. why? His flesh was no good to me. I would tell him; your flesh is no good. I pray God bless him today. He tried to explain why he didn't want to pay her and he went to jail for it. I told me it's too late. God had revealed him to me (2 Thessalonians 2:3). The judge at the court house told me come back with a lawyer. Keep this in mind please. The Judge was a woman and Mr. X had a white woman Lawyer. Muslin didn't like white people at that time. They said they were devils. They put our black people in slavery but you see I never was prejudice. I love and care for everyone that God created. My God, Jesus Christ loves all and hope no one perish (2 Peters 3:9). I was in trouble I thought. The Judge and the woman Attorney were friends. They showed their friendship at the hearing. (Now keep this in mind). The Judge was black and his Attorney was white. I said that only because he tried to teach me to hate white people. I guess by getting a white Lawyer in his mind was a good thing but what a surprise they got. When I saw him with his Master The Devil-as he had taught me. I needed My Father Jesus Christ to be My Lawyer for me.

Time round up and it's time for court again. I brought a friend with me. God had her to teach me how to evangelize. This sister was so powerful in evangelizing that I would go to church with her at 7pm and get out church about 10pm. We would stop on any corner and talk to people about Jesus. We wouldn't stop talking about Jesus Love until 12 midnight or 1am in the morning. I remember saying I can't do this 3 to 4 times a week. I was gaining strength and learning at the same time. When we got in the court house. I noticed that his Master the white woman Attorney the Devil; he taught me was there. She was very mad looking. The Judge was late coming and I was crying. I was crying so much that the court aide gave me tissues to wipe my eyes before the Judge comes in. I must have used up 12 tissues. You know they gave you 2 at a time. Once you blow your nose it's over. I was crying that much the court aide kept giving me more and more tissues. The court aide sits me in the witness chair to be questioned. She asked me who was my lawyer, and I said Jesus (I had a lawyer they had appointed to me but didn't need him). I was crying so much that the aide said Ms. Linda; after giving me more tissues to blow my nose do you need more time? She said again Ms. Linda are you alright and do you want to continue. She said I am trying to get you to stop crying before the Judge comes in. Well that couldn't happen because I just kept on crying. His white Attorney (the devil as I was taught) (which was not true and how Jesus taught me the different) said to him is she stupid, is she a real woman. I just looked at her because I saw her in the Spirit-Bowing to the God I serve (Jesus). It's time for the Judge to come in. At my surprise and theirs too; the Judge was a black man and not that black female she knew. She didn't know him but I did through the Spirit of God. The sound of the Judge voice made me feel like God had sent him just for me. I still was crying a lot. The Judge said are you ready Ms. Linda, and I said yes. His Lawyer interfered and said she doesn't want to use the lawyer that was appointed to her. The Judge said I am talking to Ms. Linda. I told the Judge that I didn't want anything he had. I just wanted my house I had purchase and is still paying for it. The Judge said did you want wife support and I said no. The Judge said I see you all have discussed the child support, and I said yes; still crying. His Lawyer was making me out to be a horrible woman. Mr. X was the one who beat me, on drugs and had and having other women as he told me. The Judge had his Attorney to be quiet. After the Judge looked over all Mr. X processions he said Ms. Linda I never met a woman like you before (his lawyer called me stupid and unreal). You don't want anything; who don't want anything from their spouse? What about his RIA's and houses (They was brought without my name on them but the law said they were mines too). The Judge said over and over Ms. Linda I never met anyone like you before. I replied; Your Honor I just want peace (I had made a promise to God and I kept it). I told the Judge he can have everything accept the house I brought. The Judge said if that's what you wants Ms. Linda it's good enough for me. The Judge said I will make him pay child support, he owe you that much. Then his Lawyer said that he wanted his name back. He doesn't want her to be Linda X any more. The Judge said that's up to Ms. Linda if she wants to do this. I said yes Your Honor he can have his name back because My Father Jesus has already given me a name. Your Honor he can have everything because God told me that one day I will have it all.

That's how I am a Great Woman in Jesus. Not a great Woman in the Muslim Religion. That is how I became ¼ of the Woman I am today. PASTOR ELECT-LADY. TO GOD BE THE GLORY.

Word of Knowledge Keep your name God gave you. There is Power in the name of Jesus. Just image how powerful your name is. WHY? Because you're Gods' child. I was ready to surrender to God without worrying, wandering what's next (1Corinthians 7:32-34). I just wanted to please God, Jesus, My Lover, My Doctor and My Lawyer.

CHAPTER 7

---⬡---

50/50 Chance   Strange Women

I really forgot to tell you about the time I had a quick decision to make. LIVE OR DIE. I am not going back to far. I don't go backwards. I just want to tell you about the Power of God. I learned about God from personal troubles; how great Jesus is. I was living with Mr. X at this time. We use to be broken up so much I can't remember the good times in our lives. Meaning; I just wanted to leave. My Dearest Mother-in-law would tell me some things to say and do. While she was putting me on his mind to come home. Remember; he couldn't go to her house because of her husband wouldn't allow it. At this time in my life I had taken very sick. Mr. X had met a lady around our house through me and they became friends. They thought I didn't know, but his mother taught me to look out for things like this. She had dealt with women like this before. I had been working but I had been so sick for months. I couldn't go to work so I lost my job. I started receiving food stamps. At that time you got a medical card also. The medical card was like an index card and paper food stamps were given in those times. In order to get a medical card you had to get food stamps. I needed both of them. I did what my Mother-in-law taught me. Don't tell them your husband lives with you. I was taught to lie (Let me say this while this is in my heart; please try to understand). I learned though the Spirit of God that some evil things are taught to us. As for children they are pure until people teach them to be defiled. (Example)

Love is either given or not. Love teaches some to love others and how to hate. Lies are taught to us. While lies becomes a part of our lives. You only need to lie in different cases is taught also. The children grow up and lie about what they think is good and sometimes they lie on everything. The color of the skin is taught to children. They will play with a purple boy or girl if they play back. If they like them they will become friends (sometimes forever). We teach color skills on all children and some pet animals too. We teach all children to fight and beat up other children. We teach them at a very early age. We would say to our children when you get to school (nursery or pre-k) today you better fight back. Hit them back and punch them hard so they can cry. Now our children become other children bullies. I mean; teach them the way of God (Peaceful and Loveable). I was taught to lie and to hit back harder.

She told me don't tell them nothing they didn't ask you. Don't give them what they didn't ask for? In reality I was telling the truth. Just for example: do you have a Husband? I would say; no an Abuser. Does anyone else live there besides you and your children? I would say no because I might see him for minutes to Spit Spirits in me and then leave. Sometimes I would never see him. I really wasn't lying I thought, but I was. (Thank you Jesus).

Every six months you would get called in for food stamps and medical cards. It was a very cold October in New Orleans, La. I believed it was the worst (1986). I was so sick that I couldn't eat, sleep, talk or walk very well. I met a lady down the street from my house. She would come over to see about me. She would come a lot but never saw my husband. Then one day she saw him and he saw her. I believed the lust in them rose up. She would come over even more. I could hear her asking the kids for me. At this time I had (2) two girls and they were able to give me something to eat and drink. I would hear the girls tell my neighbor that I was lying down or just watching television. I heard her say that's okay. I never knew that she would be sitting down with my so call husband at my house. They would be having conversations and laughers. Day after day I would get worst. My Husband would come home to just take a bath and leave. His Mother had to do everything before her Husband got home. When her Husband got home; no company was allowed, and no noise was allowed. I couldn't bring the kids by her to watch them because he would be coming home. She had no time to help me; her time was given to him if he was home. I didn't know Jesus at this time. I just remember what my Mother-in-law taught me. Just say Jesus (3) three times and he will come and help you. I did this day after day. Remembering that it is the end of October and my medical card will soon expire. My medical card expires on November 1, 1986 or you can say after 12 midnight of October 31. 1986. I had been going to my Doctor for weeks. The Doctor said you are not pregnant and he had run all kind of tests. I said he could not find out why I still was bleeding. Three months had passed by and I still was bleeding heavy. I was getting weaker and weaker. Every week the same old story was told to me from my Doctor.

My neighbor came over again, but she didn't ask for me. In other words I saw her and she didn't see me. I knew the grass had to be cut but I couldn't cut it like I use to. I heard a Lawn Mower outside in the back yard. So I look out the back door and guess what I saw. My neighbor and husband were holding the handle of the Lawn Mower together. Pushing the Lawn Mower over the grass together laughing happily until they saw me. I said it's going take both of you all to cut this grass. She said this is my Lawn Mower and I was showing him how to work it. I was so sick I just said okay. Then I said; I think he knows now. What do you think neighbor? She replied; yes; I guess you are right. She didn't come inside by me but that was okay. I had made up my mind about what was going to happen when I feel better (Of course, we think like this). I was going to beat my neighbor up and not him. That was wrong, but I didn't know that at that time. I went back and laid down in the bed. In the next (3) three hours in my sickness I heard people talking in my living room. I got up and was walking slowly to the living room. I saw my neighbor and my husband talking and laughing with or to each other. I had remembered the story my mother-in-law told me. The story about Strange Women. You see; my neighbor was a strange woman to me. I told my husband to leave and let me talk to her. Believed it or not he moved fasted. Just maybe I looked like I meant business. I was tied, sick and weak. I began to tell her the story. Would you like to hear this Story?

26

Strange Women

Strange Women only wants what they can get from you. It could be Your Man, Your Children or Your Money. I begin to tell her that when we met we became friends. Friends that can trust each other. It's said; that sometimes after a while your friend becomes a strange woman. I guess neighbor you wants to know what's strange about them and who are strange women. Now when I met you as a strange woman your conversation was very good. Then when the strange woman met your husband his conversation becomes more powerful than yours. These women always lose because they always get beaten down. I said now neighbor I think you are a strange woman. So before I could finish she ran out my house. I believed she left him alone. I didn't hear or see any more Lawn Mowers. She wasn't coming to my house anymore. God was protecting me then. The next day was on a Sunday, October 31, 1986. I was saying to myself I hope my husband would come home. I was going to the hospital and tell them I was having a miscarriage. That's what came to my mind. I felt pregnant but I was bleeding too much to be. So it was about 2:30pm when Mr. X came home. It was Halloween Night and he said; it's Satan's' night. I was glad he came home out of Satan's night. I called my Sister-in-law and she called a friend to bring me to the hospital. I got at the hospital about 3:30pm. I told my Sister-in-law and her friend that I was going to tell them I am having a miscarriage.

They finally called my name to see the Doctor. They ran tests on me and called for my Doctor. They put IV'S in my hands for fluids and also a Blood Machine too. I was getting medication to stop the pain. I was going in and out of sleep because the pain was leaving. My Sister-in-law and her friend left about 6pm. I said Thank you and tell Ma (we called my mother-in-law Ma) I will call her later. I told them to tell Mr. X to watch my children for me. A Doctor came in the room about (5) five hours later. He said to me Ms. Linda you are pregnant in your left tube. The baby inside your left tube has turned purple and it had been there. He said Ms. Linda you have a choice to make. **Have the surgery (it is a 50/50 change to live) your insides are poison. If you don't have the surgery you shall surely die.** At this time it is 11:45pm. My insurance will expire at 12:01am. So oh, oh that's all I would say. Dr. D came back into the room. He called the surgical team that was there already. They had just finished a surgery (look at God). Dr. D came back into the room to talk to me about the surgery and my decision.

Dr. D saw me shaking and trying to say the Lords' Prayer. My Lord and Sheppard and I shall not want. I was shaking uncontrollable and saying the same things over and over. The Lord is my Sheppard and I shall not want. You see; I didn't know God. I would hear my Mother-in-law say those words when trouble comes. I didn't know that it was The 23rd Psalm. I just was trying to say it. I just know I had to make a decision on my life and fast. Dr. D said I will be back. I was still shaking and asking the Jesus I heard about to him me. I ask God to give me a sign to let me know if I should have this operation. Now it's exactly 11:55pm and my insurance goes out at 12:01am and I had to make a decision. To trust in this Jesus I heard about or just give up and die. Dr. D came back to the room dressed for surgery. He saw me still shaking uncontrollable. I still was saying the Lord is My Sheppard and I shall not want. I also was saying Jesus, My Lord please help my body to stop shaking. Dr. D said to me; don't ask God to stop your body from shaking in the operation room but ask God help my hands from shaking in the operation room. I just got out of school and you would be the first one I do this operation on without help from other Doctors. He told me to ask God not to let his hands shake in the operation room. I looked at Dr. D and said lets go. I said to him I just talk to God and asked him for a sign. Dr. D and I knew God sent him. I began to say; I believe you know him for yourself. The operation took 3 to 4 hours long. So Pastor; what are you saying? I didn't know DR. D but what I did know that he was talking about God, Jesus and The Holy Ghost. They are the only ones who can save me and let me live. I could tell somebody who don't know him. That he knows you; just let him know you need his help. He will teach you about him. He is a God that when it's impossible with men it's possible with him (God) (Matthew 19:26) (Mark 11:24) (John 1:12). The surgery was successful. While I am writing this to you I am crying. Just thinking about who we serve (A Great God). He helps us when we don't know him. We need to believe what we have heard about him. Thank you Jesus for loving me. Dr. D removed my left tube and the modified baby.

Now here comes the Devil. I remember lying in my bed when my

Doctor came in. They couldn't get in contact with him. Dr. D was the Doctor on call. I thank God for Dr. D and for him answering the call.

So my Doctor comes in and look at me. At this time my Sister-in-law and her friend came to check on me. This must have been about 10am or 10:30am after the surgery. I was still under pain medication and very tied. My Doctor said to me I heard you are going to sue me. I looked at him with death in his eyes (Eyes are in large and showing no regret) and I said Doctor I have no plans to sue you. Dr. D told me that my Doctor should have founded this out before it got so far. Dr. D said a serum pregnant test as well as urine test should have been done. My Doctor was a man who drinks a lot. As I was told and witness it for myself. He would talk to you; you could smell the alcohol from his breath. I heard he's always doing something wrong. He repeated himself over and over about was I going to sue him. Saying is going to sue me. Never said Ms. Linda how are you feeling, or explain the surgery or anything. He just wanted to know if I was going to sue him. Then the God I didn't know spoke through me (I believe this). Words came out my mouth that said; (Now remember I had been under a powerful life or death surgery, very weak and not alert) I have no intention and no desire to sue you. I promise you this Doctor R. if you let me live; I will not sue you. We had been going over this for about 15 minutes or more. Then finally he said I will let you live. I hope you have a word cause if not; then I stopped him. I said I swear to God (not knowing that I am not supposed to swear) I will not sue you; just let me live. He then called the nurse in and gave her orders for me. I lived again through the grace of God. I walked out that hospital after 7 days stay. I raised my hands and said Thank you God. I got a new Doctor and never went back that way not even for my checkup. Six months later I heard he did the same thing to another lady and she sued him for millions for neglect. I heard he lost his license for a while. Thank you Jesus for loving me. I didn't need his money; I just needed Jesus.

CHAPTER 8

---◦---

God of Children

After the divorce I had one daughter who left me and went to stay by his sister. The other two was with me. Had one in the 11ᵗʰ grade and one in 3ʳᵈ grade. They both were able to experiences the Power of God. The one that was in the 11ᵗʰ grade was always in trouble at school. I use to go to an Lawyer office because I worked for him part-time. I would see this school called L. E. Rabouin Memorial High School. It's now call International High School of New Orleans. This school was for kids who I thought wanted to be somebody. I believe they taught this at this school and it was not easy to get in. I would look out the window while waiting for the Lawyer. I would point my finger and lift my hands up and say; in the name of Jesus I claim this school for my daughter Je. She was a very smart girl, but her environment had to be changed. At this time I was just a Babe (maybe 6 months) in God. For about 2 months; every time I would go to the Lawyer office; I would do the same thing over and over and would believe this. Then in the 3ʳᵈ month of the school year I received a call from her school. The principle said; we are suspending your daughter from this school. I was saved, a babe in Jesus but believed in God a lot. School had already started at Rabouin. You had to take a placement test to get in. I said; I trust you God and had to walk in it.

I went with my daughter Je to talk to the principle there. The Principle began to tell me and my daughter that it was too late to get into the school. She said; that she had not taken the placement test. I let the Principle continue talking. Then it was my turn. The principle had a Doctorate in education. Her name was Dr. Co. I said to her; Dr. Co God told me to come over here and speak to you. He told me to tell you to give Je a change to get help with her life. I told her that Je needs a New Environment and I believe through the Grace of God she will make it (my daughter was going to jail at the school for fighting). She would be in a fight every week. Then Dr. Co said let me see her grades. I brought her report card with me. She had D-D, D-D, D-F, D-F, and F-D. Her grades are first and her behavior second. The Dr. Co looked at me and my daughter Je and said; I am not supposed to do this but I will let Je in the school. I will let her choose a Career Class. If it's too late she will have to choose one for next year.

(Dr. Co had spoken Faith in my life. When she said she can choose one next year if it's too late). I send those words back to the pit of hell; proclaiming she will be back next year. Dr. Co told Je don't tell anyone how she got in. She will be on 6 months' probation and no more fighting. That school was a blessing from God. Je was able to get into the Cosmetology Classes and she loved to do hair. When my baby got home I could see no fighting-no fussing-just enjoyment was in my baby voice. Je proved to Dr. Co that she deserves to be at that school next year. My baby graduated with Academic Awards. Her behavior was an A in all her classes. Dr. Co gave Je the name Most Improve Student. Dr. Co said that Je was the Unbeliever Student. Dr. Co told me how a boy wanted to fight Je but Je came to her and told her about what happen. Je told Dr. Co she didn't want to fight anymore. Now Je wasn't scared to fight; she fought anybody at any time. Through my beliefs for my daughter and Prays to God that he honored. Je also gave her life to God. She got into the school that she thought she could never be qualify for. Now this was a Powerful thing God did for her and me. (**Peace; I Called It).** I ask God to give me peace. So he took my daughter from an environment that was filled up with not caring attitude people. That anger rules and fighting was the way to survivor. God moved her to an environment where God rules and abound. Dr. Co was a saved woman working for Jesus. She was giving the children his love and law. I pray and hope that God Bless Dr. Co where she may be. By God putting Je there where he ruled; she began to see the Power of God. I would like you to know that you, I and others can do all things through Jesus Christ. I didn't know Je always wanted to go to that school but God did. I didn't have to wonder every day, all day until she came home from school about what happen. Didn't worry about the police coming for her and putting her in jail for fighting. Thank you Jesus for loving me and Je (Philippians 4:13).

Everything was looking up and I was looking up too. I began to Preach for Jesus. I don't know where I got this song from. I mean; for about 3 months I would sing it. When I would go out to preach the Word of God I would sing this song to others. If I would go to Lafayette Park to ministry to the homeless people. Men, Women and Children; I would tell them about Jesus and how powerful his love is. Now in October it is Satanic Worship month. By this I mean; this was the month they would sacrifice people to the Devil. One time I brought Sis. Mary with me to Lafayette Park to ministry and to give out food and clothing to them. A lot of them had No Love, No Peace, No Joy and No Hope. They would drink a lot of alcohol and would get drunk. Some would do all kinds of Drugs.

Now the Satanic Worshippers (The Devil Workers) knew this. Most of them that are homeless are their choice but some has no choice. The Satanic Worshippers would sacrifice a body every day (night) in October. I would go with the Angels of God. I wasn't afraid because I believed in Gods' Word that I have Power over Satan, His Angels and Workers. I testified this at Church but they didn't want to believe this. Sis. Mary wanted to challenge me on this. At one Friday night service Sis. Mary asked me when I was going back to minister in Lafayette Park again. I told her I am going tomorrow evening and I asked her if she wanted to come. We made plans to meet in front of the Park. The Park was a cover up for the rats that live in it. (Thank God for a Place to live). Sis. Mary and I met at the park and began to minister to the people. God had me to form a circle with the people. You would really be surprise how many people would come to the circle for pray. Some came for pray and some came to get food and clothes we had to give away. As the circle is formed and God began to minister to them and telling them how to look out for each other. Then the Satanic Workers came to the Circle but couldn't come in the Circle of God. They began to tell me things about my pass. People were given their lives to Jesus, saying the Sinners Prayer and the Devil was upset. They couldn't get anyone attention so they left (We Thought). Sis. Mary was very frightened but I wasn't. After the people received their blessings from God we started walking out the Park. Not knowing that the Satanic Worshippers was waiting on us. They were dressed in the Devil uniforms that identify him. The colors that were on their lips and hair were purple, red and black. Some had all the colors and some had one or two of the colors? The leader came to me and said do you want cigarettes or do you want money to go gamble. At this time our cars was park outside the Park by them. I just believe God blinded them so they couldn't do anything to our cars. I began to tell Sis. Mary to go get in her car. She said Evangelist what's going to happen to you. I told her that God is and will protect me. I told her the Satanic Workers knows me because they see me every time I come here. The Leader said to me as I was walking to my car that he will get me. He said I promise you I will get you. You see; the Song that God gave me I would sing it to them. It might just help you as it has helped me and so many other people. It Goes Like This.

Long, long time ago; my heart was in trouble with sin. My head bow down in sorrow. The Devil had me wrap in sin. I had a hard time seeking salvation. I had a hard time resisting temptation but I kept on searching. I kept on searching; until I found King of Kings. He changed my feet so I could walk right. He changed my mind so I could think right. He changed my heart so I could live right. He was my Doctor on the sick bed. He was my Lawyer in the court room. I want to say yes, yes until I founded King of Kings. I kept searching for him (Jesus) King of Kings until you find him (Matthew 7:7).

I remember when I started going from Church to Church. Meaning; going to my church and then visiting other churches after my church was over. It's okay but you need to ask yourself what you are looking for. I didn't know what I was looking for. One thing I knew was that I liked the Praises, Worships and the Word of God that kept me feeling good. Me and my youngest daughter Jo had been to one church and were going to another. This church was across the canal (we say this in New Orleans). The church was over at 3 pm but was having a revival at 6pm that same night. I and my daughter were driving from church, when it started raining. It was raining so hard and I was driving faster than I normally would have. I wanted to go back to church. I was driving fast because I just wanted to get us some chicken to eat and get back to church. While me and my baby girl was driving in the hard rain I saw a car look like it was slowing down. I just kept driving at the same speed while praising God in the car. You see; God had been teaching me about obeying the law of the land. I heard God and didn't hear God. Look like I was gaining speed on that car. I thought the car had slowed down but it had stopped and was just sitting there. It had emergency blinkers on but my car was going so fast I couldn't stop it. I knew me and my baby girl would be badly hurt and even die. I began to put on my brakes and began to hug my baby. Turned lose the wheel of the car and covered my baby head. She was in the front seat of the car with me. It was not mandatory to wear seat belts then. (Loving your children but not believing this could happen to you).

I began to call on Jesus in a Voice of Distress. I called on Jesus like I needed him right away. My eyes were closed and I just knew me and my baby died. I continue calling on Jesus with everything I had in my Heart, Mind and Soul. When the car (talking about mines) stopped; I looked and my car was on the side walk. My car was placed on the pavement by the angels of God. The people who had saw what happen said; you are lucky. They said we never saw anything like that before. Are you or your baby hurt? You didn't hit the car. I never saw that before; they said this again. Saying your car and your baby is alright too. The people began to say Powerful. I just got down in the car and glorifying the God I now was serving. I had just started with Jesus and he saved our lives. MY baby and I were kept by God. We started glorifying God and thanking God over and over. My baby said to me; Mama did you see what I saw (I thought I was the only one saw something powerful). What did you see? She said a big white hand placed our car on the side walk (pavement). I said to her yes; it was the hand of God's angel who helped us. I told her the Angels of God saved lives for Jesus. From that day forward I decided to serve God. (Psalm 91:11). By believing in Jesus Christ and not his god. Mr. X would not give me any money. Before serving Jesus, he would give me little money but it stopped. My baby girl had a Doctor appointment. I had no money but my middle girl God-Mother was a nurse at a Doctor office. She let me bring my baby in for sore throat. I had about 75 cents for a loaf of bread. I had some tuna fish at home in the can to fix. I didn't have no bread or anything to drink besides water. I didn't want to ask his mother for anything. I had Jesus now and I started having Jesus as my best friend instead of her. I asked my Jesus to help me. At this time my baby girl needed to bring a plant to school the next day. The other kids in the class had already brought their plants. She said she knew I had no money so that's why she didn't tell me about the plant. Friday morning was the last day to bring in the plant. I had only a half of a day to get a plant with no money. I called her father and told him and he said no, he wasn't giving me any money. He said you are calling this man which is a prophet; God. He isn't the only begotten Son of God; now ask him. I said nothing to him but just continue believing in Jesus. We had a long wait because I had no appointment. She gave me one off the records but not a paying appointment.

There was a man that came to the doctor office passing flyers out. It read the Funeral Home is giving away bedding plants for Mother's Day; come and get one. It also said it was Free while supplies last. I said to my middle girl God-Mother I was just thinking where and how I was going to get a plant for tomorrow. I began to cry and thank God';not knowing if I would make it there before they closed. I was hoping that all the bedding plants wouldn't be gone. Now remember I said I had no money. I put 2 dollars in the gas tank to get the doctor's office. I needed bread and something to drink. My friend said all she had was a dollar. I was able to get my baby medication for free. She gave the dollar to me and I was able to buy bread and juice for my baby. **God will supply all your needs. (Philippians 4:19).**

Before we go any forward. When I got saved my girls saw Jesus work in my life, in their life and they got saved too. They would worship God with me and without me. My baby girl spoke in tongues and wanted to be a Pastor. She played real church with us; she was the Pastor. I made a strong fall in God. As you continue reading you will see why they dislike me still yet (Pray for them). I was the strong man of my home (Mark 3: 27) (Matthew 10:20-22). So Blessed; Praising God in my Heart, Mind and Soul. Not afraid to tell my middle girl God-Mother about Jesus. On the way home my baby and I went to the Funeral Home to see if we would be able to get a free plant. My baby needed it for tomorrow morning when she goes to school. I got there and I saw at least (20) twenty bedding plants sitting on the steps of the funeral home. A lady greeted us and you could hear in her voice the Spirit of Kindness. She said to me and my baby; pick any one you want. The lady said because all of them are free. My baby picked the one she wanted and we said thank you. I told the lady; I know this is God. How I didn't have any money. How God blessed my baby and me and the lady just smiled. I had been there talking for a while and guess what? I didn't see anyone else come there while I was there to get a plant. **God Won Again** in my life and my baby life too. For what my baby said to me when she got home was how beautiful her teacher said the plant was. My baby was so happy with a smile so happy. I saw the Power of the God me and my baby was serving.

CHAPTER 9

Keeping your Eyes on God

Something when we See, Hear and Taste the Power of God we still don't be completely ready to serve him. What do you mean by this Pastor? I mean; we know that Jesus loves us and has compassion on us. He always comes to our aide. I am talking about us as Babes and long timers in Christ. He will come to our aide if we just believe who he is. We just take it for granted. We praise and worship God when we feel like it. Not when God is calling us to do it at the time he wants us to. The Spirit of Self-Righteousness comes on us so fast. When we witness this Spirit in someone's life who is serving God. We can't see behind their close doors. Just the open doors that they kept open for us to see. Do they respect and praise God? yes I beleive they do this all the time when God calls them. Well; some do and some don't and I am one who sometimes does that. Putting one eye on God and the other eye on the Devil. (**Lets Tell The Truth?**) The Bible says: As Jesus speaks: (Matthew5:29). And if thy right eye offends thee, pluck it out, and cast it from thee: for it is profitable for thee that one of thy members should perish, and not thy whole body should be cast into hell. I was one who didn't keep my eyes on Jesus and Jesus only. I began to put my eyes on lust. I started looking at movies, where men and women held hands. Men and women were kissing in the mouth. They would go out to dinner and made each other laugh. Now I am making an excuse but what can I say. I kept looking at this, saying to myself I always wanted to have that kind of love in my life. Knowing; Jesus can do this for me. If I just ask him and believe him he will do this. We began to say; I am not going to tell my Father I want a man. A man to give me a ring, open doors for me, hugs and able to spoil me. A man who would surprise me with different things. All the while I knew God can do this. He did it for so many different people. I can't believe he will do this for us.

One day my Mother and Aunt came by my house with a guy name Mr. O. I wanted a ride uptown and Mr. O agreed to bring me. While riding in the back seat of the car; I could see him looking at me in the rear view mirror. He was smiling and saying to himself thank you Jesus. At first I thought nothing about it. When he dropped me off, he gave me his phone number. He said call me and I will come back to get you. I didn't call him because I was so afraid to fall. After being faithful to God for (8) eight years I was afraid of men. So now I title this: The Love That Healed Me Is the Same Love That Destroyed Me.

I worked at night from 11pm until 7am on Sundays throw Thursdays. About (3) three days later (after meeting Mr. O) my baby said somebody was at the door and his name is Mr. O. I was in the bed at this time and it was about 9pm. It was time for me to get up any way. I told my daughter to ask him what he wanted. He replied; I brought her some food to eat before she goes to work and a diet coke and a little Debbie cup cake. The next night he did the same thing. He kept doing this from that Monday until that Thursday. He left his number with my baby to give to me to call him. I called him on that Thursday night. Thanking him for being so thankful and kind. I told him I will be off from work on Friday and Saturday nights. We talked through much of my lunch break. On that Friday I let that Deceiver in. I started minister to him about Jesus. Really giving him what he came to do for the enemy (Devil). All I knew was how he made me feel. It was like no other fleshly man had. By just taking time out to talk to me. He would tell me things that no other fleshly man would tell me. He wasn't afraid to be seen with me. I didn't know why he wasn't afraid or embarrass to be seen with me. I had very Low-Esteem because of all the abuse that I went through. I thought I was ugly and not worthy to be with anyone. I married my first boyfriend and the marriage was controlled and rejected for (24) twenty-four years. I was good enough for him to use but wasn't good enough for him to love me. Mr. O told me and showed me that I was good enough for him (I thought). Mr. O told me he had just came home from prison after doing (3) three hard years. He said while he was in prison he prayed for a woman like me. Now you better believe; the Devil entices men or women to become that man or woman you have been waiting for. Look how Adam was so lonely and wanted companionship. The Devil used his companionship to eat off the tree God forbidden. Just think what the Devil wants to do to you. He would play my favorite game with me all the time (dominoes). While playing dominoes I noticed that he hated to lose and be laughed at (the fun of the game is bragging). I would win and laugh at him and say, how are you going come to my house and bet me (not so). I noticed he hated rejection (Well we all have little rejection problem but he had a lot). I saw this and pretended that I didn't notice or see this spirit in him. That's how we get in trouble with God and with ourselves. Compromising with people seeing and not seeing who they are and what they do. Mr. O and I became great friends, lovers and liars. You see; I call myself ministering the Word of God to him but I let him ministry and show me his god (Satan). By this I mean; I would over look things he did and believed everything he said. Keeping Jesus in my thoughts but yet listening and pleasing him. Mr. O was the loved that healed me of my vision of having a man on my side. Having a man to spend time with and for someone to share your emotions too. **I give to you this Advice (Wait for Jesus).** He will give you your heart desires. Once you allow Jesus in your life then you will understand what I am saying. **(Matthew 6:33) it says; But seek ye first the kingdom of God and his righteousness; and all these things shall be added unto you.** But we don't want to seek God. We just seek him or her (your mate). We only seek God when we are in trouble. Only when we can't pay our rent, lights, phone bills and car payments. But to seek God for our lives that he desires for us it's a no, no. We seek God when we have made up minds on what we are going to do. We have made up our minds before we came to God. We would say God lead me or tell me it okay. We didn't want to hear or pretended we heard God speak and say no. We would say it was the Devil speaking because our minds were already made up. Well that's what happen to me. I had a made up mind to make Mr. O my lover. His mind was already made up to get me and destroy me for the Devil. (Now just listen! I gave Mr. X in the divorce all the property we had and IRAS' also. I kept the family home because my girls needed a place to live. I didn't know it was God then but I know now it was God who blessed me and my children with a brand new house. People would talk about me and him all the time. Saying things like how could Linda mess with a low life. He's a no good dude and she will see how no good he really is. Well I began to see that. Years before I met him I visited Atlanta Georgia. I really liked it and I told my cousin that one day I will come to Atlanta and live there. I thought about moving to Atlanta with my baby girl and Mr. O. I thought it would be a better life for us. He pretended that the decision was on me but he encourage and worried me about going. My baby girl cried and cried not to go. She had to go because she was under age to stay with her sisters. I decided to listen to him about how he loved me and how we were going to get married. That we were going to start a new life in Atlanta together. The new life part played out in a few months. I sold my house in one week after reducing the price so we can go to Atlanta. My house was worth 110,000 I sold it for 85,000. Now tell me how the Devil had me? Got rid of a blessing that God had given me and my children for a piece of flesh. We moved and everything was okay for (4 – 5) four to five months in the new city. A new life (I thought) and a new man. I would go to the corner grocery store to play casino games for money. He would be so anger with me. He thought I would lose all the house money and he wouldn't have any money to get high with. He was on drugs like my Ex was. Before we left New Orleans I brought a car from his brother for him. I had the titles of the car put in his name instead of mines. I wanted him to know how much I appreciated him for being there for me. Well of course; the wickedness of getting off on me with my money enter into his mind, and that's what he tried to do. We got a job from my cousin R to paint the inside of a house. Him and I would go to the house every day and paint a little. One day I noticed drug dealers across the street from the house seating on the porch. He promises me that Atlanta was his new start of life and no more drugs for him. I saw him talking to the drug dealers and I said I see you have not given those drugs up. You are still lying and stealing from me (Meaning; my love from God). I stopped going to the house to help him to paint. The owner of the house had given us a $700.00 check as the down payment on the painting of the house. He gave me the check and I put it in the bank. I gave him $350.00 and I kept $350.00. That was not good enough for him. As I am thinking now I had $28,000 when I went to live in Atlanta. Less than (6) six months; my money was gone. I did no drugs but yes played the machine but not like that. I know

now how much I loved him. I became blind at the tactics he was using against me. He was going to the bank and taking my money from me.

To God be the Glory!!!

I got a job at the Race Track Gas Station. I was really glad not to go and paint with him anymore. You see; He knew I was trying to get connected again with God and his Angels. I know now that I didn't have to try so hard I could have just ask God to forgive me and he would have. I said the Sinners Prayer over again and repented. A little advice I give to you (Please turn from your desires and addictions, the kinds that make you unable to stand stronger in God). I noticed that Mr. O would come home as a man I never knew or wanted to know.

His skin had turned darker and his words had become a weapon against me. I wouldn't say anything to him. I would just go to sleep early because I had to be at work early at 5am. Leaving the house at 4am, I had to go to sleep early. It was summer time and my baby went to New Orleans. The next couple of days I saw his friend from New Orleans at my house. He was one of the friends who he did drugs with and who was a great painter; I heard. I spoke to T and Mr. O said that T will be staying with us in the guess room until the painting is finish. He said he came to help me finish and I replied okay. That night T and him smoked drugs all night and drink beer. They were playing and singing loud music. I woke up about 2:30am or 3am and I could hear T saying, please man. Then T said man don't hurt Linda, I didn't come down here for that. T was saying man let it go; please man let it go. I could hear him saying to T, man you don't have anything to do with this. I heard T say, man if you do this I am going home I promise you. He replied it's going to be okay. I thought I heard correctly but it was so early in the morning. I was woken out my sleep ; you know how it be. He had never really hit me hard but tried once in New Orleans when his sister stopped him. I stopped speaking to him for about (3) three months. He asked me to forgive him; I did. I went back to bed and then the alarm clock went off. I got up with the Spirit of Death on me. What is the Spirit of Death? It's a feeling like; you feel like you don't want to be in this world no more. You feel weak in everything you try to accomplish. You became a failure. You feel like crying and crying because you will miss your family. You are very Nerves, Fearful and Hopeless. So that morning I started crying and crying saying, oh my God. I still knew God but I was not serving him I had stopped. It had been at least a year since I served God. I got dressed for work. The doors to get out the house were blocked. The front door was blocked by choice with furniture. The back door where my car was park was blocked with Mr. O body. He was sleeping across the back door. Whereby; if I attempted to open the door it would hit him and wake him up and I didn't want to do that. I knew he had been drugging and drinking all night. So I began to pray, asking God to make a way for me to go to work. I couldn't miss work because I had just started and they were training me. So I would try to walk over him lying on the floor. It didn't work; so I just kept praying to the God. The one I once loved trusted and believed in to help me. I knew God was the only one that could make it possible for me to go to work. The Bible says (Mark 10:27) with men it is impossible, but not with God; for with God all things are possible. Once you have tasted and seen the Power of God you will never forget it. So it is about 4:45am; still crying and believing in Jesus. He made a turn from the door and crushed over like a new born baby. I was able to get out the house and go to work. When I got to work I told my boss how I felt death on my life. I kept crying over and over and my Boss told me to go outside. Get a cup of coffee and a cigarette and rest your nerves. He said nothing is going to happen to you. My Boss said Mr. O will take care of you. He didn't know it was him that I was talking about. So I stood outside for about an hour and smoked a lot of cigarettes and drink a lot of coffee. I finally stopped crying and went to work. Now those things I didn't helped to calm me down but the Prays that I lifted up to God gave me the Peace I needed.

You know our Father Jesus Christ knows the different cries we make to him. Every different loud noise we make he knows it's us and what we are asking him to do for us. Now after surrendering to God again; saying the Sinners Prayer, repenting and letting God Love me again; I felt Peace. While at work Mr. O pulled up at a gas pump to get gas. This was about 11am that same morning. I wouldn't wait on him because we were told not to wait on family members. My Boss, a talkative co-worker, I and God were there. I was not going to be a part-taken of his sin this morning

(Stealing Gas). HE was so mad with me I didn.t know what to do. I remember one time somebody left their credit card at the Gas Station. I gave it to Mr. O and he would by Gas, Cigarettes, Beer and what every he wanted. It had to stop for me, so the answer was no. I had rejected him in front of his friend and I knew he was mad but how mad I didn.t know. I knew the love he gave me fleshly was good and secure for me (I thought). He came inside the Gas Station and the talkative co-worker waited on him and he put $5.00 of gas in his car. I knew where he was going at; that the gas was just enough to go there and to get back. I felt better after he got his gas and left. I told my boss if I don't come to work tomorrow send the Policeman to my house for me. Well he laughed as if it was a joke but it wasn't. I got home that evening I took some New Orleans shrimps out the freezer to fix Jambalaya for him and his friend. I also through the Spirit of God put color in my hair. I said through the Spirit of God because I was very tried and sleepy from crying all day. I heard a voice that said put your color in your hair now not tomorrow. The voice said it will be pretty so I agreed and put the color in my hair. Now us who dye hair know that we put a little dye on our eye brows also. While standing by the sink in the kitchen next to the stove and refrigerator dying my hair. I heard a car door shut; I knew it was Mr. O. and his friend. He came into the kitchen through the back door and my Spirit jumped with Fear. He looked like he had lost everything he had and was very upset. He looked at me and said give me some money. He began to curse me out but I said nothing. I just began to pray under my breath to God. Now I had left God for a long time and choose him over God. I knew that God will never leave me nor forsake me. Meaning; that God will always be our Father and when we call on him he will answer (Hebrews 13:5). Now the second time he came into the kitchen he looked at me like he wanted to kill me. He had a lot of hurt and hate inside of him. He had begun to cut the grass in the back yard of our house. Then he came in the house looking hateful saying I am going to show you something. He said I gave you all the money and you spent it. Now remember I had just sold my house, brought him a car, clothes and brought him to Atlanta. He had nothing when he came to Atlanta. I thought when we meet unsaved people we can help them to change. That's not true at all; only God can change them and us. Mr. O knew God enough to help others if he wanted too. He said he needed a change in his life so I thought that a new environment could be very helpful. That's what I did and it is a no, no. I gave him things he never had before and treated him like somebody you love. Being polite, kind and mindful of his feelings and so on. Well that doesn't work; please trust me on this. I know only one who can change you or him or them is JESUS. He didn't want to change just pretending that he wanted it. I not only wanted a change but a needed a change. Once you know God; you know who's the Change Master Is. He began to say things under his breath. He always speaks to you or people with his fingers especially when he is loaded. Well he was loaded, so that means; his fingers was doing the talking. His eyes were protruding hate. He got some water out the refrigerator and saw the Fear I had on me. I believe unto this day now – If I had not let him put Fear on me or see Fear on me; I believe that he wouldn't done what he did to me. So he returns back outside and I heard him talking to his friend and then I heard the Lawn Mower starting up. While standing by the sink in the kitchen. I heard voice say, take the color solution off your eye brows and wash them. I did as I was told. When I finish washing my eyebrows; I heard Mr. O coming in again for the third time leaving the Lawn Mower running. I kept the color in my hair because my hair had not finished coloring. He came in and when I turned and looked at him, I just smiled. I smiled and hailed my hands up because he was going to kill me. So when I did that he hit me so hard in my eyes. I felled between the sink and the stove in the kitchen. He started beating me like he was beating on a piece of flesh, or beating all the hatred inside him out. I start asking him not to kill me. Then he began stumping me until he broke my right side down. He broke my Right Jaw Bone, Right Wrist, Right Thigh and my Right Ankle B. Both of my Eyes were closed and I couldn't see any more. I still was crying out saying; why Mr. O, why Mr. O. Please don't kill me. He began to put me between his legs and hit me harder non-stop. **Then I heard a Voice say, you are asking the wrong person not to kill you (Mathew 10:28).** And fear not them which kill the body, but are not able to kill the soul; rather fear him which is able to destroy both soul and body in hell. When I heard the voice say this, I knew it was God. Then I began to say **Lord I repent; help me father. Why have thou forsaken me? Help me Father and I said it again and again. Why have thou forsaken me? Then I heard the voice of God say, (just stay with me) don't worry**

about what he is doing to your flesh. HE said stay with me and I said okay Father. So then when he began to hit me; it sounded like thunder. I began to look as I was instructed by the voice of God to do so. I saw the hands of God as he was hitting me. He was hitting the Hands of God and not me anymore. He began to punch with everything he had. I wasn't feeling anything anymore. He continues punching for a while and got much tied. He said; oh you are not going to cry anymore. I will show you something just wait and see. I was under the Wings of God. You See; I couldn't feel what he thought he was doing to me. So he started stumping me again. Then I saw the Hands of God go under his feet and flipped him over. It was like some men picked him up and flipped him to the floor. But it wasn't any man it was Jesus. He heard **My Cry**. Now Mr. O stands at 6' 5" and I guess he weighs about 230-235 pound. So when the Hands of God flipped him over the Angels of God lifted me up. The Angels said to go to the back door your neighbors are out there wondering what's going on. They have heard your cries. So when I went to go out the kitchen back door he got up. He said I will kill you. He began to pull my head back as I had my hand on the door knob. Remember I still had color in my hair. So when he grab my hair his fingers went straight through my hair. That when I began to open the door and my neighbors was outside waiting for me. I remember the Paramedics came for me. I saw Mr. O cutting grass in the back yard like he had done nothing. I began to hear my neighbors say they didn't know he had beaten me like that. He was arrested and had no remorse in his face or voice for what he did. My Daughter and her boyfriend who had come to Atlanta wanted to kill Mr. O friend. I beg them not to and then they told his friend to get out and walk to New Orleans or get there the best way he knows how. Through the Spirit of God I talked to them and I allowed him to take the car I brought for Mr. O to New Orleans and give it to his father for me. The Father refused to give the car up to my daughters. The Father knew that it was my car but I guess as the world say blood is thicker than water. Then months later the car burned up by its self I heard.

CHAPTER 10

Blessings in Disguise

My daughter and I went back to New Orleans, Louisianan. The Spirits that once destroyed and ran me away was waiting for my return to destroy again. Well at this time I was force on the words my mother said to me. How much she cared for me and how much she wanted to help me. Maybe it was true in her mind but it didn't happen. I was about to receive unemployment checks. I received them about (2) two weeks after I lived or moved in her house. At the time I lived with her I had to sleep on the floor in a vacant bedroom that had nothing but junk in it. My Mother said she wanted her stuff and don't touch it. When my first check came it was about $125.00 a week. My mother wanted all my food stamps and ½ of my check every week. I said to her that I was trying to get me a place to live. She began to call me all those names that she always called me (Stupid, Ungrateful, Mother f, Whore and Kiss and Eat my butt). Now at this time I am lost in the Mind, Heart and Soul. I know I wanted and needed Jesus. I thought I needed my Mother to just love me one time in my life. Really loving me with no strings attached. The first week I gave her $100.00 out my check. The second time I gave her $75.00 out my check. The third week I gave her $25.00 out my check because a Reality Company was going to give me a one bedroom apartment for me and my baby. I was going to become his Manager for the apartments. I used to manager Coronet Court Apartments. The man said I needed $250.00 deposit. I had saved $150.00 and I needed to give him this $100.00 that I had left from my check. In the meanwhile; my food stamps came for me and my baby girl. They sent me $351.00 of food stamps. So I gave the food stamp card to my sister and mother and told them to only spend $200.00 so I can had some stamps for me and my baby when I move into my apartment. My sister N told my mother to spend all the food stamps since I was living in her house. I just cried and couldn't believe that they spent all the stamps. This a Friday and the Super Ball Game is coming on Sunday. It's (2) two days before she spent all the food stamps. Not knowing but should have known that my mother was having a Super Ball Party. When I received my unemployment check she wanted $75.00 to buy paper supplies for the Party. I told her I didn't have that amount to give her at this time. I heard her say to my sister I am going to put her out. Well I heard no more noise after I gave her $25.00. It's Super Bowl Sunday and people are coming to her house for the Party. My mother said to me (I can't remember what). She just wanted me to say something so she could say get out. I remember saying; WHY? She said I can't stand you and I want you to leave my house now. The people that was on the sofa kept their eyes on the television station waiting for the game to start. The people pretended that they heard nothing. I began to cry and my body was so tied. I was hurting so bad because I had to sleep on the floor in a vacant room with little cover. Please help me Lord as I am crying now. I went into the room that had a lot of stuff in it to get my suitcase and an old trunk. The men and women that was at the party saw me trying to lift those things up. They refused to get off the Sofa, Love Seat or Chairs to help me. I went to get my car and drive it upon the grass closer to the door. My niece C who was about 11 or 12 year old helped me lift the trunk into the car so I can drive away. Now at this time I was lost. They kept my baby girl; Thank God for that. It was me; the Devil wanted to destroy and is still trying to destroy me. I had nowhere to go. I went to Harrah's casino and slept in the bathroom overnight. I played a little but my mind was on finding a place to live. I saw an older lady playing a machine in the Casino. I began to talk to her and she told me about Crescent House Women Batter Shelter (Batter Women Shelter). So I called up there and spoke to a lady name Ms. C. She wanted to be call Ms. C and she would call you somebody else name not yours. Thank God for Jesus changing the times in people lives. I spoke to Ms. C and she told me to call tomorrow morning because first come first served. I had been at the Casino going on (3) three days and I needed a shower and some rest. So I called a friend and ask her if I could stay by her house but that didn't work out so I went back to the Casino. When 6am came the next morning I called Ms. C. She told me a lady is leaving today. Can you get here by 8am this morning? I answer yes, so I got there at 7am because I was already uptown Waiting and Excited and Thankful. When you get like that you want to tell somebody that God Has Won Again in your life. Arriving at the shelter I waited downstairs; just waiting for the lady to leave. Ms. C called my name in the office and asked me some questions. I got in and I just got to tell you who was in my room. I desire to tell you this because all kinds of people are batter. I use kinds of people and not color of people because batter and abuse has no color. A Drug User, black female that every time she did drugs she would want to defend herself against anyone who is near her. She would steal your life if you left it behind. She had a bad Spirit of Fear. Now a Gay, white female who was so sweet and kind. A girl who was a cheerleader and who had it all going on; until she got raped and turned gay she said. Her Gay Lovers would beat her mentally and physically but she was my friend who I liked a lot. We were not lovers just friends. I could trust her about my life. she wasn't no different from me. we both and all of us were battered. There was one that was from the South Pacific Islands. She was an Madamenoire (a woman who entertains males and females with whips, clothes and sex toys to freak them out). She would make a lot of money. She came to the shelter from being abuse by your husband. There were many more; especially one calls Ms. E. who thought she knew the Universal. She thought she knew the styles of people life but not her own life. I gave example of them who was with me. you see; being batter or abused it can make you become what you don't desire to become in life. Please believe this; its really true (ask someone who has been abused or batter or who is still getting abused or battered). God touched their lives through me. We think we are put in places to be Destroyed but we are put in place to be The Destroyer through the Grace of God (Hebrews 4:16) (2 Peter 3:9). We all were in this Batter Woman Shelter trying to survive. We were Batter Women who need help to get some rest for a while, food and shelter. Until we decide to let Jesus in our hearts, minds and souls again or for the first time.

I could remember I use to go to Lafayette Park to ministry. I would ministry to the Lost, Homeless, Hopeless, Batter and Hurt People. I told you early in the story it was one of my missions for God. Not knowing

I became what I used to do for Gods' people (Comfort, Love and Teach them about him. TO GOD BE THE GLORY).

So I went to sleep early the first night. Took a shower and washed my dirty clothes. The morning came and I had to see the Psychiatry (Psych) Doctor and of course Ms. C was waiting to talk to me. Ms. C got rich off us at the shelter. The supplies that were given to the shelter were offered taking home by so many people like Ms. C. Well when you wake up late the kitchen is closed. The refrigerator locked, freezer locked, panty was closed and locked. I didn't know this is what happens when you wake up late. I had no choice as Ms. C thought; when I got up I saw a bowl of cold oatmeal with no milk or sugar just paste like, no toast or juice. I asked Ms. C who is this for and where is breakfast. She replied to me; that's for you and you should have gotten up earlier to get something to drink. I replied to Ms. C I don't eat oatmeal. She replied eat it or don't eat. So I sit there crying from about 8:00am until about 12:00 noon. I was rocking backwards and forwards saying I am hungry and I don't like oatmeal. Please can I have something else to eat? She said; no and I couldn't understand that. By sitting there so long I asked God could you please help me. I am not only hungry but sick too. Look like when I finish praying a Nun Sister M walked in the Dining Room where I was sitting. She said what the matter Ms. Linda. I began to tell Sister M what Ms. C had told me. I also told Sister M that I was not only hungry but sick in my mind, heart and soul. So she asks Ms. C. about this and she told her the same thing I had told her. Then Sister M got angry and told Ms. C to open every refrigerator, freezer, pantries and unlock everything that's locked including the cabinets. Sister M began to say this is food that was donated to these women and they can have it if they want it. So Ms. C was so angry with me but I paid no attention to her. I started to look for something to eat but everything was out dated (not exaggerating or making it up or lying). I mean; out dated by 2 to 3 years old. I boiled me 2 eggs and had out dated toast and water to drink. Later that night Sister M called for me and asked me how my breakfast was. I told her how everything was and I told her how the frozen foods, can goods and etc. were out dated 2 to 3 years old. Sister M said to me I will call a meeting tomorrow at 3pm. I will put the announcement on the board and everyone will attend this meeting including Ms. C. We had the meeting and in the meeting Ms. C couldn't answer any of the questions. She was quiet and had hatred toward me. Sister M asks me if I would clean out the freezers, refrigerators, closets cabinets, etc., and get all the out dated food out. She said get some young ladies to help you. We cleaned out the refrigerators, cabinets, freezers and etc. We took 15 large trash bags of out dated meat, cereals, can goods and snacks etc. When we were finished Sister M said to me Ms. Linda would you like to be over the kitchen. I said; yes before I knew what the duties where. My duties were to ask the women what they felt like eating. Make a Grocery List, Make Menus for Breakfast, Lunch, Dinner and Snacks. Make Duty List on who will cook Breakfast, Lunch, and Dinner. Tell them what time Dinner was to be done. Every Saturday we had more groceries including meats and ice cream coming in. The God of Abraham, Isaac, and Jacob not only delivered me from starvation but made me the leader of the kitchen. God gave me knowledge about what to do and how to feed his people. I just wanted was to eat breakfast. Giving All Glory, Honor and Praise to the Most High God (Psalm 118:22). The Stone which the Builders Refused is become the Head Stone of the Corner.

When kind things were taken part in my life, I thought I was getting well. My Counselor thought I was smart because I would write down my feelings and still do write down my feelings about a lot of things. Sometimes I would walk in the back yard of the Shelter and listen to Ms. K calling some people or everybody Vipers and how she hated them. You see; I had been touched by God and I couldn't hate anyone. I just hated the Spirit of the Devil that was in my life. Sometimes I would walk by my friend A and look into her eyes of emptiness; not knowing what's next. I thought I was getting better but actually I was getting sicker. We got a new lady Ms. F who didn't like me. Why? I guess just the way I look crazy but looking like I belongs to God. She would make a different between me and the other ladies. I had been going to the Doctor because sometimes I would think about how I was beaten and how I left God. One day I told my friend A that life is not worthy. I never told her I was going to kill myself but she knew it. She told me how she use to say things like that. So that night I went to my car not knowing my friend A was following me and I took a handful of pills. My friend A ran and called Sister M for me. They rush me to the Hospital and I became a Mental Patient. With Major Depression with Psychotic Features-Post Traumatic Syndrome (meaning;

a person who had been in War or in a bad Fight). At times I could never forget. I became an Experimental Patient, who is fighting for their normal life to come back or not to leave. I was put into the Hospital for about a month or more. I was so sick I thought my name was Jane. You see; Jane was the Spirit of Hurt, Depression, and Hopeless that lived in my life. I will tell you a little more about Jane later. Now living at the Shelter gave you the release of the Spirit of Fear temporarily until you leave the Shelter. We had only (3) three months to be at the Shelter but some of us needed more time. We didn't know the man who shelters all his children; Jesus is that man.

After trying to kill myself again and failed. The Devil that encourage me to do it, failed too. God let me live again. As I lived in the shelter the Spirit of Fear came out me for a season. When you began to listen to Gods' voice and decisions for your life you will have peace. The Devil will leave for a season and but he will come back and you will be ready for him. The Devil said this about Jesus too (Matthew 4: 8-11) (Luke 4: 2-13). Here I was in the shelter with women who I thought was in the same condition as me. Remember there are people who are in worst shape than you; so please help them. These people have no Hope, Joy, Love or Peace. Never believed in God or wants to believe in God. There is something special when you let the Love of Jesus in your heart, mind and soul (Try it you might just like it). When you start feeling love and hope for others that you don't know God is very pleased with you. I understand the Scriptures about Love Your Neighbors as Yourself (John 15:10). You see; I tries to keep Gods' commandments which are to; Love Him with all thy Heart and with all thy Mind and with all thy Soul. Thou Shall Love thy Neighbors as thyself (Matthew 22: 37-39). Also check out (1 John 4:7) and (1 John 4:11). I know now; how many people in the world is hurting and can't find Love, Peace or Joy for their lives. The Shelter was a blessing not only for me but for others with and without children. A Shelter for Gods' people to be safe. A chance for them To Find Him, To Learn of Him, To Trust Him and To Love Him Back. Some of us do this and some of us don't. While I lived with many of the Mothers who batter their children; not all but most of them. The children Mothers were batter and probably thought they would treat them like the way they were treated. Whether it was Mentally, Physcial or Controlling its call; Abuse. In The shelter there were a lady that had three children; two girls and one boy. Yes; I was sick but I know the signs of Abuse, sick or not. If I see someone being treated the way I was treated as a child or adult; I felt their pains. The woman would treat one little girl and boy different from the other little girl. She would talk to her (cursing and screaming) and would beat on her all the time. The other (2) two children were not treated bad or beaten like the other little girl. So being over the kitchen I would have television popcorn nights for adults on Fridays and on Saturdays for the children. When she didn't want that little girl to come but let the other two come I spoke to her about it. She told Ms. F who didn't like me about what I said to her. Ms. F told her that I was making trouble with her. I began to tell Ms. F how she was treating the children. She told me to mine my business because they were her children and she can do what she wants to them. Well; right there I knew Ms. F didn't know about the Love of Christ. Some of the ladies agreed with me and some agreed with Ms. F. So I knew who knew God and who didn't. In my sick mind I would cry out for all the children in the shelter. Also I would cry out for those who were with other family members. Every night I would cry out for the children and their batter mothers at the shelter.

God gave this to me. (Please just listen) I would say this so they could hear me.

Darkness-Darkness

Darkness-Darkness when does the light comes in. Some abused women lives in darkness. Abused women live in their past hurts and sometimes their present hurts. Those abused women never wants to come into the Light Of Love, Joy, Peace and Happiness. Those abused women Cries for help in a Controlling Way. WHY? Because they have allowed the Darkness to Conquer their lives. This Darkness is passed on or into their children lives. Children who are victims of an abuse from the darkness of their Mothers. I would ask God to help us who is living in Darkness with our Fear and Hopeless. Sometimes we try to Look for Light but Just Not Strong Enough to Continue the Search. Now some abuse women just keep looking Into the darkness of their past with their children. This became a Prayer to God at night before I went to sleep.

Now this became a Prayer for the children of an Abused Mother. I Hope and Pray that this reaches somebody's' heart. Let Them That Has an Ear Hear What the Spirit is Saying. To God Be The Glory!!!

The Cry of an Innocent Baby

Darkness – Darkness Please leave; so that those innocent babies can one day come into light?

Eyes – Eyes Please Open Up

Hearts – Hearts Please Pump Gods' Blood of Love

Arms-Arms Please Hug Those Innocent Children of Darkness

Tongues-Tongues Please Praise Them and Speak Positive Things to Those Innocent Children of Darkness

How Many Eyes Are Open How Many Eyes Are Open Is It Just Mines Or Is It Just Gods'.

Let us as abused women realize that abuse lies within us and not in our Innocent Children. The Cries are getting Stronger for the Innocent Children of Darkness. Because they are Crying Out for Help. Crying to Come Out of the Darkness with their Abused Mothers. God Can Do – God Will Do – God Shall Do What his Word Said. Blessed the little Children (Mathew 19:13-15) (1 John 3:18). Let Us As A Family Destroys The Darkness. Let Us Come Today Into The Light Of Love, Hope, Peace And Joy In Christ Jesus.

I wrote this Parable to let us as Abused women know that Abuse lies within us. Sometimes we don't realize that we Abuse our Children and might not want to do that. But it happens sometimes and we got to pray to God that it doesn't happen. All our Anger, Hurts and Pains that lies in our lives need to come out but not on our children. So Pastor; What is Abuse To Children? Well Abuse is talking to them any kind of way. Cursing them, Talking in a Controlling way. Making them be who you want them to be and not realizing that it is Abuse. Not always giving them Presents (Gifts) and not your Presences (A little time together). Demanding them to eat what they don't like and making them eat it all. Well some of us have the sense of taste. The ones who does had the sense of taste, doesn't like certain foods. (Think About This); That's why different foods, like Ice creams, Cookies, Sodas, etc. was made because certain people like certain things.

Please always remember that we are talking about our children. They Are Just Like Us, Just Smaller. Meaning; they were born with their likes and dislikes feeling. You can hurt their feelings like they hurt yours.

Stop hurting your children.

So let say this again. When this is said my eyes began to fill up with tears for the Abused Hurting and Hopeless Women. Who has been Batter and who still are being Batter and their Children? When God gave this to me at the Shelter I read it at our Thanksgiving Dinner and Christmas dinner Party. Some of us were selected to speak; I was one of them (Look How God Works). After the Spirit of God allowed me to do this I notice the children were treated different. In a more Loveable Way (I mean; no more names called, and no more beating and punishments were taken place). I heard their Mother said to all her children how much she loved them. I hope through the Spirit of God; that this would just hit your heart, mind and soul in Jesus name. So if I was you but I am not you; I would listen to the Parable again. To God be The Glory.

Some nights at the Shelter they would talk about their gods and I and K talked about Jesus. He is The Source of our life. Finally the Non-Believers Where Believing and them that once Believed and had Faded Away, Came back to Jesus. God gave me so much Favor at the Shelter. God Is So Amazing To Me. He's A Wonder to My Soul, Mind and Heart.

While I was in the Hospital my friend A at the Shelter (I Pray and Hope I could met her again' a really nice friend) she came just about every night to see me. She was a white lesbian who was batter by her lovers. (Now just hang on in). I used Color to let you know about the kinds of people God created. It is not their Color, it their Hearts that God Has Fixed. I learned through the Power of God that he Create Different Kinds of Human Beings, Animals and so on. You see; we have all kinds of Liars; White, Black, Spanish and so on. We have all kinds of sick people who need Jesus. Different kinds of people are suffering from Depression, Abuse, Controlling and so much more. They need Jesus's love too. Jesus made all kinds of people and them too. She would come to see me at the hospital just about every day. I have to say that again to show you just what kind of person she is. One day my friend A came to the hospital to tell me about a program that helps homeless people with an income to get an apartment. She knew I was receiving unemployment; it's so powerful how God used her in my life. She filled my application out for me because I was unable to do so. I got an apartment but I was still sick. I thought my name was Jane when I got Sick (Depress, Hurtled, Rejected, or Batter). Jane was a Spirit that lived inside of me and controlled my Emotions. So the Doctors would put me back into the hospitals to try new medications on me that they thought would work but it never works.

CHAPTER 11

What Is Faith?

When the Angels of God would speak to me I would reply to them. They said that Spirit called Jane would you leave. You see; the Doctors had to call me Jane in order for me to answer them but when the angels came I understood. So when the Doctors began to call me Jane I wouldn't answer to that name. When they called me Linda I answered. The Doctors thought they healed me from the new medications they gave me. All the while it was God that healed me. He sent his Angels to take care of me. The Doctors said she is well now and lets send her home with 12-19 pills to take a day. I would take these pills and Jane would leave for a while then come back.

Then one day I decided to rededicate my life to Christ. Meaning; giving God everything. I gave God My Emotions, My Joy and My Peace (I called) to him. I Surrender my Heart, Mind and Soul to him and ask him for a Brand New Heart and Mind. I began to lift up Jesus by, starting to Dance, (Praising God) Worshipping and Talking (Praying) to God. Asking God to give me another chance to prove to him that I loved him and trusted him with my Life. Then for (3) three months I did this; not bragging just wanted a change in my life. One day after praising and worshipping God I went to the Mental Health Clinic for my (3) three months checkup. My name was called by a Nurse I never saw before. I thought well maybe I just don't remember her. Taking 12-19 pills a day depending on how I felt. If I felt weak 19 pills and if I felt good 12 pills a day. I was supposed to take 19 pills a day but I took them how I felt. So when I went into the room with the Nurse to check my weight. She also checked my blood pressure and asked me some dumb questions. She asked about my medication that I am supposed to be taken. The Nurse began to say to me; Ms. Linda you are taken all these medications and still living. I jumped out my chair and ran out the office to find my Doctor. I told him that he's given me all those pills to kill me. I told him what the Nurse had said. He told me to come and show him this Nurse. We went into the office where the Nurse was and she was gone. Dr. AM thought I was losing it. I told him to look in my chart because she was writing in it. He looked and founded the writing in it on me but no signature was there. I cried and went home to talk to Jesus. You see; Dr. AM knew I was saved. He was from South American I think. I use to talk to Dr. AM about Jesus and I want you to know that Dr. AM is saved now in Jonesboro, Georgia. That's where I believe that's' why I went to the Doctor.

To God be the Glory!!! God is Powerful; just Believe.

I went home and got into devotion with God. I heard God said **Do You Trust Me Heavenly Child and I said Yes; Father.** He said I really need you to tell me the truth. I said yes; I trust you. Then God said stop taking all those pills. He said just take (2) two pills a day (1) One Zoloft and (1) Trazodone and take no more. Jesus began to say I will heal you and I will give you a whole new mind. God told this to me and really I believed God had been trying to talk to me. So he sent an Angel to talk to me and I heard the voice of God. I started taking (2) two pills a day from 12-19 pills a day for (1) one month. God said after one month stop taking those pills. After God said that to me ; I said Father I can't go to sleep at night. You see; God knew what I needed. Jesus told me to go the Doctor and tell her that you can't sleep at night. I did what God told me to do and the Doctor gave me 2mg of Valium to take to sleep at night. I went to the Doctor every month for (3) three months to get the Valium. The Doctor said she couldn't give any more after the third month because I will get addicted to them. Now it's me, my mind and Jesus. Well I ask Jesus to take my Mind and give me a Whole New Mind and Heart. He did, yes he did that for me. I testify today that I No Longer takes Psychotic Medication. I Have Been Set Free

From Jane And All Those Pills. It's going on (7) Seven Years or More since God Deliver Me and Counting.

I moved back to Jonesboro, Georgia. We say Atlanta, but it was a county in Georgia not too far from Atlanta. So I had to go to court for Mr. O beating. The Judge called me in her chambers and asked me how much time Mr. O should get. I told the Judge give him what God said. The judge didn't like my answer. She thought I stilled loved him and was fearful of him. All this she said was true. I wanted her to give him what God tell her. I really wanted to kill him in the court room but I Thank God for Sending His Angels To Minister – To Me (Luke 22:43). The lady Judge chose to postpone the court until next month. I had begun to forgive Mr. O because my God teaches me how to forgive them that hurts me. GOD will forgive me for hurting him (Being Disobeying).

(Luke 6: 32-36). It was court day and I still believed then and believed now that Mr. O is one of Gods' creation (John 10:16). Me and my neighbors arrived at court early that morning. The court sent my neighbors a suspender to come to court. The court was going to pay them for testifying. When we got to court, they called my name and my neighbors in the court room and they told us he took a plea bargain one year in jail but I heard six months. In Georgia you do 2 for 1 meaning (2) two days for (1) one day in jail. I was pleased because that's what God allowed him to have.

Still living ½ and ½ in God. Healing is a process. I still was feeling Hurt, Embarrassed, Loneliness and Fearfulness; even though I believed God. You know sometimes we be with God but not in God. By this I mean: we say we understand God but really we don't understand. Now when this happens; ask God to teach you what he means. Say God give me your Wisdom and Knowledge so I can really know you (1 Timothy 2: 2-6). I decided to stay in Georgia. At that time I was getting healed from the beating and yet I was feeling very sick. I started going to Church by Pastor K, who ordained me in 2006. I still remember feeling sick but I began to let God clean my insides up. To let you know as he was cleaning my insides up I was having bad pains in my stomach. I would go to the Doctor and Emergency Room all the time. Sometimes the pains would hit me at night when I would eat different types of foods. One night at church we served pizza and I ate it. The night before I had corn on the cob and had to go the Emergency Room for pains in my stomach again. I had been there before for the same thing but this time I decided to talk to the Doctor. The Doctor came into the room and I asked him to run a Gallbladder Ultra-Sound Test on me. I don't know who but somebody told me to tell him that. God used someone to help me. I told the Doctor and he laughed and said; okay I will do just that. I told the Doctor that God leaded me to tell (ask) you to do this test. He ran the Gallbladder Ultra Sound and came back and said you have Gall Stones. He said he can see them coming out the sack (Meaning the Gallbladder) and this is dangerous. He refers me to a Surgeon who can fix it. I asked my daughter and not God what she thinks I needed to do. The Doctor I went to was so cold hearted when he told me about the surgery. I was confused and fearful when my daughter said yes, do it. I didn't ask God what to do. I told the Doctor I will get back with him about the surgery and he said I needed it. **God had not given me the Spirit of Fear but of Power, Love and a Sound Mind (2Timothy 1:7).** So I started believing this scripture greater than what I had before. This Scripture was going to become part of my life. So when you get into situations that have you to choose then search your scriptures because **Your Scriptures Are Life**

(2 Timothy 3: 16-17) (Romans 1: 17) (John 10:10) (James 3:17). Apply them to your Life every day. Say Them, Read Them, Sing Them, and Meditate on Them. You need to know those scriptures and other scriptures to give to the Devil so he can flee from you. I began to say I have Power (The same Power that was given to Adam at The Beginning of Time) (Genesis 1: 26-28). When Jesus died and rose he left us with power inside of us. (Acts 1:8) (Matthew 28:18) (John 14:26) (Luke 24:49). I began to think about the love of God and put it in practice too. (Ephesians 17:19). God taught me not to fear man but fear him (Matthew 10:28). So I agreed to have the operation. I wasn't in God but knew him and I knew how much he would love me if I let him. My daughter JN and my cousin went to the Hospital with me to have the operation. Was I Afraid? Yes! ; Was I Confused? Yes! ; Did I believe in Jesus? Yes! ; But I was so Fearful of this. The Doctor told us that the operation will take about (30) thirty minutes. Well I woke up; I guess about (8) eight hours later to found out I was admitted in the hospital. I remember waking up with two I.V. in my hands, white tight stocking on my legs, a tube in my stomach and hot with fever like firer. So I ask my cousin who stayed with me all that time to tell me what the Doctor said about the operation. She said the Doctor told her that my Gallbladder was Gang-Green and has Poisoned My Insides. He said I don't know how she is still living but I knew it was Jesus who kept me. I stood in the hospital for (7) seven days.

God won again in my life.

The message behind this is if; you ask him to heal you and believe he will do this for you. You must believe who Jesus is and who sent him to help you. **He is a True Doctor who has never lost a Patient.**

CHAPTER 12

Returning Home

Then I started fooling myself.

My neighbor told me about a **Chat Line**. This line was for lonely people, and I agreed to get on it. I called and met a lot of Satan's' people. Their Minds and Hearts were on destroying people. Converting them to their Pleasures and Ways. I would call every night instead of reading My Word (Bible) to talk to Satan's people. When I would get off the Chat Line I would ask God to help me. I said to God I don't know what's happening but all I know I am being drawn in. One day I called the Chat Line and talked to a man name was John (Not lying this is the truth). God was in the mix because there was something special about Johns' voice that I couldn't or I didn't want to stop listening to. Every night John and I would talk and if I missed him he would leave a message in my box to meet him at a certain time on the line. I decided to give John my home number. We would talk every night at about 7pm and he would talk about his mother all the time. You see, I hated my mother but he loved his. He would say how he would take care of her when she was with him. He had to put her into a Nursing Home because he couldn't no longer take care of her. He was reminding me about Love and how it Heals.

I didn't know he was talking about the Love of Jesus but every day I waited to talk to John. He never talked about sex or any other horrible things that was not of God. Time passed; I would say about (6) six or (7) seven days and I didn't hear from John. He also gave me his home phone number but John and I never met just talked. I would call John and he wouldn't answer. One night after so many nights passed John answered his phone. It was a Saturday Night when he finally answer his phone and I was so happy to hear his voice. I didn't know what to say but Thank You John for answering your phone. I ask him was he and his Mother okay and he said yes. I then asked him where have you been that I have not talk to you. He said Linda when you don't hear from me I am spending time with God. What you mean by this John. He said Jesus is my life and without him I can't do anything. He said when I spend time with God he heals me. I didn't know John was or is one of Jesus Sheep's. All I knew he was kind; speak with love in his voice and is my friend. We talked for a long time. That's when I broke down and began to cry. Saying to John; I remember when I use to spend time with God like you. I told John how much I missed fellowshipping with God. He said; Why not try it again. I am going to Church in the morning John because I need Jesus. We said good night to each other. I got out the bed right after I talked to John crying so much and began to find something to wear for Church. I woke up about 9am and Church started at 10am. So I laid back down for a few minutes. I tried to get out the bed to get dressed but I couldn't get out the bed. The Devil had me pinned down to the bed. My body wouldn't or couldn't rise up. I began to ask or call on Jesus to help me get out the bed. I remember saying to Jesus please help me to put my stocking on my legs to go to Church. God sent his Angels and they helped me to get out the bed and dress for church. I went to church and began to praise and worship God. I didn't want the Chat Line anymore. No more smoking, gambling, cursing, sex, no evil people in my life and I stopped speaking evil things about people. I still wanted to be accepted by my Mother, Daughters and others. I would go to church and praise and worship God so had I would get sick. I would dance so hard they called me The Dancer. While I was at church doing worship I would do a War Cry. It's hard to explain but I would open my mouth with a yell like I was capture and was trying to get loose. On Sunday I would do this War Cry. I did the War Cry for the next thing about three months. I spoke to John and he was pleased. Then John phone was disconnected and until this day I haven't spoken to John. I would like to tell him thank you John for Loving Jesus and for Sharing His Love to Others. I would forget about me when I get into praising and worshipping God. The Pastor of the church called me to his office and ask me who I was. I said a sinner and he said you are more than that. I have heard your War Cries. Please tell me who you are. He said I want you to be an Associate Pastor here. I told him I couldn't because I was sick. He said you don't sound like you are sick but I said I was. He tried to convince me but I told him I was full of demons and I don't want to pass them to others. I told him I need help myself. I will let you know when I am ready.

I started waking up every morning before I eat and worship, praise, prayed and talked to Jesus. I did this for about three months. In between that time; I had two friends. One as my lover and the other my friend. My friend would take me out to eat, buy me cigarettes and give me money because he wanted to be my lover too. I looked at him as a great friend and he was. I would curse him out every time he would tell me about being my lover. So since I devoted my life back to Jesus. My friend saw a change in me. I will never forget his words he told me. He said I know there's a God but I never saw a person make a 360 degrees turn in their life like you. So you see; my friend was letting me know I was coming or belongs to God again. He said you don't' curse, smoke or anything anymore.

I loved to shoot pool in the Sport Bars and I let that go for God too. The other one (The Lover) didn't believe that I stop playing pool. I called the Lover a five minute man. Five minutes to take his clothes off; In five minutes the sex was over, and the next five minutes he would leave. I would just take it being so lonely because I was not looking at Jesus just my flesh. You see; some things are good to you but not good for you. The Lover wasn't good for me and it was Choosing Time (The Lover or Jesus). Test time came after my morning devotion to God. The Lover knocked on the front door. I heard he told people he can get me back. One thing I remember; the Lover would always tell me that I was different from his other women. I said; what you mean? He said your heart is different from my other women. Well he didn't lie but it was different because I had let the love of Christ In. The lover knocked on the door I didn't answer it the first time. Jesus told me to answer the door; that's the Lover. I could hear the Lover on the other side of the door saying BABE this is me, let me in.

Then The Test Began. I started crying and crying loud saying; God please don't let me open this door. God is saying open the door and the Lover is on the other side of the door was saying the same thing (This is me babe let me in). I couldn't because I wasn't strong enough. I still was weak for the five minute man. The Lover continues knocking and hearing me cry. He began to say what's wrong; why are you crying? Let me in now. You might not think five to six minutes are long but it is. It can kill or destroyed you or save your life. I had made up in my heart and soul to love Christ and no one else. I continue saying to Jesus; please don't let me open this door. I am not ready; please, please. I heard Jesus say okay but he will be back and what will you do. I said I will open it then because I will be stronger in you. I will be able to resist lust of the five minute man.

I told this Parable to let you know how we feel or when we are not strong enough in God. Please let me give you some **Advice.** Get stronger in God before you make the wrong decision in your life. The Lover left but came back two weeks later. I let him in and shared the Sinners Prayer and told him about my life in Christ Jesus. I never messed with him anymore and nobody else. **Gods' Love Healed Me Again and Didn't Destroy Me.**

CHAPTER 13

---◦◉◦---

Higher Heights

So after three months of devotion with God (Exactly three months). I wrote down the time of Rededication, October 25, 2009 and this was January 25, 2010. I was finishing up with my morning devotion with God. I said to Jesus (I had just finish cooking my grits, eggs, and toast for breakfast)(after devotion you are very hungry) I am going to sit down to eat my food and I will talk to you later. I put my plate on the table and **I heard God say; I will Sup with you this morining (Revelation 3:20 – 22).** I begin to hold my head down and cry. I can feel his presence of God and I was crying so hard, so hard that my tears were falling like a river. I heard Jesus say; why are you crying Heavenly Child and I said who can withstand the Power of you. I continue holding my head down and crying. Then Jesus said to me; **Now Everything You Always Wanted to Know About Me You Can Ask Me.** I don't remember anything else. When I woke up I was in my bed. Got out the bed went in the kitchen to get something to drink. I saw my plate for breakfast still in the same spot and never been touched. **I Say This To You; When You Give God Devotions Every Day He Will Take You To A Different Place In Him.** He will Teach you more and more about His Word and about His Truth.

I go back to Church still doing War Cries but different War Cries: Cries of Victory. Seven months passed and I was ready to talk to my Pastor (October 25, 2009 to May 25, 2009). I went to him and told him I was ready to become one of his Associate Pastors. Then he began to say you are a Prayer Warrior, not a Pastor. I had been a Pastor since 1998 but never walked like one. We went go with this for minutes then he said okay. He took me downstairs from his office into the Church were his Congregations was and introduce me as a Pastor. I served under him for about a year until jealousy set in (Proverbs 6:34). I continue in God but let my Emotions set in again. When this happens to you; do what the Bible says in (Colossians 3: 2-3).

CHAPTER 14

That Night I Died

At this time I had to be an Overcomer of this Powerful Spirit of My Fresh and Affections (Emotions). That was a Battle for me because of so much hurt I have been through. My emotions for my Daughters, Mr. X and my Mother had to be healed. I changed my phone number and thought it was the right thing to do but it was not. I thought I had forgiven them and forgot about it but I didn't. I would pray for them but not Honest. I wanted them to Pay for what their Love had Cost me. God wasn't pleased with my actions, thoughts or believes. I had some Dreams and a Vision that came Alive. Before this Powerful Vision came, I would give my friends the Sinners Prayer and didn't care what they said about me or did.

The First one was a dream. I was with some Sisters and Angels and I saw Pink Shoes, Blue Shoes, and White Shoes. I remember having some shoes like each of them. The more I saw them the more I remember those special shoes I once had. I tried the Pink Shoes on and they were so big. I tried the Blue Shoes on and they were to tight. I said I had White Shoes like that before. You see; The Pink Shoes were to big because through the Grace of God all my Troubles were taken away with the Help of Giving Jesus my Life. The Blue Shoes was tight because I was holding on to a lot of Hatred I thought was gone. A lot of Bitterness, Pain and Fear was still inside of me. I didn't have enough room in them to walk like Jesus wanted me to walk. Now the White Shoes; I remember having them at one time. When I wore them; they let me know that I was Walking Righteous and Holy with Jesus. I started Crying saying Jesus Please Help Me To Get Some White Shoes Again. So I got up and began to Worship, Praise, Prayed and Talked to God that morning.

I had the Second Vision and it was Real.

I was watching television when I went to sleep; I could remember; it was about 12:30am in the morning. I tell you why I said that; because when it was over I looked at the clock and it was about 3:00 am in the morning. I said I Died and I believe that. I was in the room with my daughter JN and her baby (She has her now but not then), Mr. X and others in a room. JN was combing her bay hair I could remember. I saw JN, Mr. X and Me running in a Green Field. A Beautiful Field like you never seen before. This happen on March 30, 2010 ; returned back March 31, 2010. JN baby was born on October 16, 2013. (She has a Powerful Name). As the three of us was running in this Beautiful Big Field Full of Beautiful Grass and Trees I saw a Big Angel. I thought it was a Giant Man. As we are running and trying to get away; this Man in White Linen was so Tall I could only look up at him. I only could see a Gold Belt around His Waist but I never could see his face. He would run in front of us and say ; **I am The Death Angel**. We continue running, we ran so fast until we stopped. He appeared and said **I am The Death Angel** and I have come for you all. By then we knew he was telling the truth. I don't know how we got in these chambers of Judgment but we were. We could not only see the chambers but there were other people there who were sitting on the left side of us. The Judgment Bench was on the right side. I could hear people talking but I can't remember who they were. The Death Angel took my daughter JN first. Stood her in front of the Judgment bench and lift his hands up and his voice up to Heaven (I say Heaven because we recognize Heaven as something above). The Death Angel was talking to someone about JN (For I saw no Scroll or anything). I thought I heard that Voice That The Death Angel was talking to before. I was so fearful and emotional. I can't remember the people on the left side who were talking too. The Death Angel talked to that Voice for about a minute. Then I saw them, I say them, I can't remember who they were but they took JN down a long Hallway; not really dark but semi (dim). I was crying so much (I am a Crying Prophet) that the Angel told me to stop crying, I cried the more and it's Mr. X turn. The Death Angel did the same thing with him but I stood in front of The Death Angel as The Angel pulled a Scroll out and began to read it to the Voice above. Then I recognized that Voice ; it was the Voice of Jesus. I began to say, Jesus, Jesus I want you. The Angel said to me again, be quite but I couldn't. The Death Angel continues talking to Mr. X but I didn't know what he had told him. Mr. X was standing there for about five minutes. They came and got Mr. X (Can't remember who they were) and he also went down into this Hallway. It looks like a Holding Place but better than a jail. It had doors, lots of doors with a little light in it but not dark. It's now my turn. I couldn't remember them that were behind me that sit on the left side that was talking. I stood before Jesus with The Angel. The Death Angel pulled out a Scroll; My Scroll was kind of long. I mean longer than JN and Mr. X. The Death Angel was talking to Jesus about me. I was crying; saying Jesus can I come by you. I wanted to come by you Jesus. I said this but they continue talking. They talked about me for about five to ten minutes saying things about me. Still pleading to Jesus to come by him. Then the Death Angel stops talking to Jesus. I said to the Death Angel what did Jesus said about me coming to him. The Death Angel said Jesus will send you back to Earth and I said why? **The Death Angel said your Works are to Great For Hell Holding Place. They are to Great For Death Holding Place. So he will send you back so you can get yourself together to come to him one day.** So I will bring you back for now. When I got back home; my television was still on. I saw on the television a Beautiful Blue picture of the Sky. I saw water and I could hear **The Death Angel say; Give Glory to God. (Revelation 20:12-15) (Revelation 20:6-8).**

I shared this Parable with you to let you know that you will be Judge according To Your Works. Rather Good or Evil. Begin to do Works that Spiritual(Good) Not Evil.

There are three holding placing until christ comes back for his people.

Hell Holding Place

A place where the Unbelievers, Fearful, Murders, Abominable, Liars, Whoremongers, Sorcerers Idolaters. Them that maketh a lie and them that has defileeth themselves. Them that worketh Abomination. Them who never wanted or never accepted Jesus as their Lord and Savior?

All false Prophets, Prophetess,

Palm Readers and Witches will be placed there too.

They that don't believe Jesus is the only begotten Son of God. Them that don't believe he rose from the dead and is sitted at the right hand of the Father. They that don't believe in His Word or do it (Ephesians 5: 1-7)

(2 Corinthians 1: 8-10) (1 John 2: 18-19) (Revelation 21:8) and (Revelation21:27).

Death Holding Place

Is a place for them that have accepted Christ as their Lord and Savior? Their works has not change from evil to good. Can't love or treat their neighbors as themselves? Them that preaches Gods' Word but doesn't live by it. Ones who heal the sick, prophecy His Word to others but yet still live in darkness. Them that give lots of money and food to his poor people but yet chose whom they want to give it to. Those that God has cleaned up from sin and they has exchanged their souls for Power and Money, Lust and Pride. Them who using the Gifts that God gave them to worship (using it for the Devil) Him. They don't do this for God and his people in Love. Only for the Devil to get Glory. Exchanging their souls for Power on the Earth. Them that are leading Gods' people in Untruth about him. Them that says Jesus to his people, and only lead Gods' people for their money and not for the love of Christ. Them that are still living in darkness and their deeds are also dark. Not Loving God with their Whole Hearts, Minds and Souls. Not Loving their neighbors as God Commanded them to do so. Them that Once Obeyed, Trusted, Loved God and his People. Denying the Power of God inside them. The Holy Ghost Of Truth) (1 John 2: 9-10 – 14-16)

(1 John 3: 16-23) (1 John 1: 5-6) (Matthews 7:15) (2 Thessalonians 2: 1-3).

Paradise Holding Place

Is a place where Jesus is. The home for all men, women and children who has been Faithful to Gods' Word in all things.

You must become an Overcomer of all Things. You must be Holy as God is Holy. Believing Jesus in all things.

Letting yourself be taught the life of Christ.

To learn and teach others about the love of Christ. Give what God has given to you; which is love and forgiving.

I know this Parable Is Hard to Believe. All I can say is to ask Jesus about this Parable. Ask Him Do I Belong To Him. You see; this is why I had to write these Testimonies of Jesus. (John 14: 1-4) (Revelation 21:7) (Revelation 22: 1-7) (Revelation 22:14). Am I so different and holy ; no, no. I just try every day to stay with the Different and Holy One Jesus. Every day I ask God to help me. Every day of our lives is different. One day it's like this and the next day it's like that. (Let me; let you in.) Every day is a new day. So the key to it is ; Live in the New Day, don't bring what took place the Day before – Week before or Years before. If I was you but I am not you; I would come into my New Day with Christ. He's a God that lives not in the Past but live in Newness Every Day and Forever. So I went and repent to my Daughters, Mother and Mr. X and so many others. To my Daughters I began to say; will you all Forgive me for not being the Mother that you all wants me to be. Not the Mother you all believed I should have been. Maybe one that I was supposed to be. Forgive me if I have hurtled you all. Forgive me for not letting you all know about Jesus Christ at birth. I said to My Mother I repent to you for all these years for Disliking you and Jealously over the Love you gave my Brothers and Sister. I know why you did it that way and I am sorry for hurting you. For Mr. X I said would you forgive me for Hating you for the Pains you caused in my life. I Thank you, because you allowed me to meet My Real Lover and Husband; Jesus Christ. I began to repent to so many that had hurtled me and them that I have hurtled.

You see; God gave me a chance to tell so many more about his Faithfulness, Truth and Love that he has for all of us. If we just let him in our minds and hearts to just love us.

I am still trying to get another pair of those White Shoes-----Pray for Me.

CHAPTER 15

My Provider

So now another mistake I made with my emotions again. I would move just about every year. Getting my grandchildren and keeping them and fighting with their Mother and Father over and over. They would fight me for the children food stamps etc. I had to go to God again to ask him to Shut some Doors that would take my Heart and Mind away from Him.

(Matthews 6:24) (Joshua 24: 14-15) (Luke 14: 33) (Romans 8: 35-39) (Matthews 10:35)

(Matthews 19: 29). I gave all that Drama and Ungodly Things to God and Left it behind me. I take my Section 8 and turned it into a one bedroom, instead of three and moved back to Georgia. I had to move out there and I moved without God telling me to go. Moved faster then I wanted to. I know what it means to move on Emotions, not on the Word of God. So me who wants to get away, moved to Georgia from the family and headaches. My daughter friend that I talk to; told me to come on. Not having a place to live or anywhere to go. So I left my furniture in storage in New Orleans and I went for it. I took some clothes and two suitcases with me. You see; **Rejection was another Spirit of The Devil that had to be destroyed by God. If I had just Trust God Enough to Teach Me How to fight** it I **wouldn't be moving**. I believe until the day I go to my home in Paradise that this Spirit was sent to Teach Me about the Power of Jesus that Lives Inside Me.

Going to Georgia ; I got my Daughter Mother-in-law to pick me up. I decided to live with her until I go to my appointment with housing.

I was not talking to my daughter and I wasn't being put out when she couldn't control me. Living in heat 90 – 105 Degrees by her house ; I remembered that. Before coming there my daughter asks me to come and help her with her son. He was out of School for the summer time. My Daughter reminds me of not coming to her 12th grade graduation all the time. She graduated twenty or more years ago. She would go to work and I was not allowed to put the Air Condition on until she got home. I offer her to pay the bill or some of it but she said no. I asked her Mother-in-law to stay at her house until my apartment came. Her Mother – in-law use to say to me; Linda I want to be like you in God. What she didn't know was that I had Thorns in my sides too. I knew she was Jealous of me for many years. When we did worldly things as well as spiritual things she would get very anger and wanted to fight me or anyone who was friends with me. I just looked over it believing she just wanted to help me. It was going on my second night there and Rejection kicked in. I was using her phone when she asked me to get off it. At first I thought she was joking but she wasn't. She wanted to fight; I was talking to another so call friend who is jealous also when she took her phone and hung it up on the other friend. She begins to push me in the closet and I said I don't want to fight. I thought you were my friend. Now I had no money, car and no place to live. So I left her house and went to the corner store called my friend Bro. RR to pick me up. I went by my little cousin who I ½ raised and her daughter put me out. I was walking down the stairs when I heard God say everywhere you go they will put you out. Are you going give up on me? I replied No; Jesus I will serve you regardless of what happens, and God said we will see. I met a lady that said she has a friend that I would let me stay by her.

I asked a friend to send me fifty dollars because I was hungry and needed a soft (cold) drink and I will send it back to him (which I did). I received the money and went with the lady by her friend house (Really she was the lady aide). She told me the lady wanted fifty dollars for me to live there and it was all I had. You see; they were working together against me. So I gave the lady all I had. I called a friend that now live in Georgia we were friends I thought in New Orleans to help me. The lady, her aide and I went to met Jy at CVS drug store. My friend Jy was buying me some cigarettes because I had no money. (Cigarettes were always my weakness when hurt comes in my life). My friend Jy came in her daughter Jaguar

Car and the lady and her aide became jealous about my friends' daughter car. I only stayed there for one day and I gave her my fifty dollars. Then they said if you have a friend that has a jaguar car you can go and live by her. That morning we had gone to Church and I let her wear my favorite shoes and some earrings. They were laughing when they said, we are going to get your clothes and bring them back to you. They did this after they got my money. Now this is the Third put out. I went with my friend Jy to her daughter house because her daughter went out of town for two days. She said I could stay there until Sunday. It was Friday evening and I was hungry and tied. I only had two days to find a place to live. My friend said her daughter lifestyle with her man wasn't for me to see. I respected that because I believed they respected the God in me. (I was in a bad shape myself). I ate and slept that Friday night. I got up on Saturday morning and my friend Jy was telling me about the Salvation Army Shelter on Lee Street in Atlanta. I called them and they told me to come in before 6pm. Well Fear set in because her grandson didn't get off from work until 5pm. The Shelton was in Atlanta and we were about thirty to forty-five minutes away depending on the traffic. Packed my clothes and was waiting for him since I called them at 10am. Thanking God and Jy for this Blessing. When her grandson got home it was about 5:30pm and I just know we weren't going to make it. Got to the Shelter at 6:15pm there were people in line waiting outside the gate to get in. ther were lots of people that was inside the gate talking, playing cards and smoking cigarettes. When I got in; a young man said to me he had been waiting on me. Now I knew when I saw the other men and women outside the gate in line and couldn't get in; it was God. I knew God still Loved Me and gave me Special Grace. The young man gave me the rules and regulations that I hard to follow. The rules and regulations were easier than I could believe. We go upstairs to be placed. Showing me my bed and locker.

All kinds of people are inside. I don't use Race, Creed or Color because they all were Hopeless, Fearful, Evil, Ungodly Confused people. He gave me a bed up at the top. The beds there were old time bulk beds that they don't make any more unless requested. They were so strong, strong with no latters to get up on the top. So I went into the television room and just cried because he gave me a top bed and I knew I couldn't get up there without help. I was old and heavy. So I just stood in the television room for about an hour or two crying. A younger lady name CR came in the television room and said what's the matter. I told her I couldn't get up there at the top of my bed I was assigned to. By being older and heavier and loving God (she said she saw Jesus) she had companion on me. She said I will swipe my bed with you. We went to the young man in the office to ask if it would be okay. He replied No; she must sleep in her own bed that was assigned to her. He continue saying; if she can't do this, then she will have to get out. She would have to get into the line and wait for a lower bed; if we have one. It was raining so hard and I saw so many young girls, older women come in after me and got lower beds. I couldn't understand that. So CR said I will help you get in your bed. She got a chair that had no back to it but just a half of a seat that was broken. I was praying and crying at the same time but CR was encouraging me how I can do it. I got on the chair but couldn't put my big thighs upon the bed. We kept trying for almost an hour. Finally, I got in the bed. I knew the Angels of God and CR helped me to get in that bed. When morning came a lady wanted the chair and came and got it. Now I am stuck up in the bed, can't get down. I saw CR and she said Mama just jump down; I will help you and she did. I don't know what they saw in me. I was hoping I could see what they saw. They treated me very bad as if I didn't belong there. No matter what they said to me; I never replied. I ate by myself. I would give my Sweets (donuts, cookies, pies etc. to the children in the shelter. They would give them ½ of a donut and they would cry to their parent or parents for more. Not knowing that some of the other women didn't like that.

I was in the Enemy Camp Believing In God. I learned Atlanta and how to catch the bus off Lee Street to the Marta. You had to get out by 6:45 no later and back in no later than 5pm if you wanted dinner. The earliest you can come in was 3:30pm. The next three days I would take my shower and talk to God. Then God answered me about why I was at the top of the bed. Believe it or not I would see a lot going on at the top. I cried every night about getting in my bed that was at the top. I used a chair and CR would help me every time. I would pray for everyone in the shelter and me at night. I over heard them talking (not all) about whom do I think I am. They wanted to fight me but I heard CR said W hy? Do you all wants to fight her? Then I heard God said I put you up at the top for your protection. I stop crying and found a way through The Grace of

God to get up into my bed (Sometimes we think the worst about things when it's not pleasing to the Flesh). On Sundays you can stay in all day if you sign up to go to Church. A man in a salvation uniform sung one song and said a few words then church was over. We praised, worshipped God and heard the Word of God in fifteen minutes (No Lying). I just stayed to myself and prayed. Smoking cigarettes one after another. One wednesday night a lady Pastor came from off the streets to teach us about Jesus. She was teaching us wrong. She said all we have to do is give God our Life and do nothing else. We knew that's not true. I began to raise my hand and questioned her Untruth about Jesus. We passed words about her teaching. I don't know what came out of my mouth but I knew it was Jesus. So when I finish talking through the Grace of God; I was so surprised. The one who really didn't like me stood up and said that lady is right. Then they began to look at me differently. They asked me questions about Jesus. Before I left I was going to have Bible Study (Didn't ask God is it my time to leave). I wasn't afraid to let them know who Jesus was and about his love he has for me and them.

It was raining a lot in Georgia. We had to get out everyday rain or shine. We would go sometimes to a another Shelter (Its' called a Day Shelter). It had no television but you can take a shower, wash your clothes (put name on list) and use the phone (5 minutes, and at a time). Free clothes sometimes and a hot lunch. In by 9am and out by 3pm. We was given four pieces of toilet paper only. It didn't matter number one or two. Your monthly or not; Wow!!! Still had to Thank God for this because I could have been outside with nothing. So for five days it rained and I was in the rain. Had no money and you can't stay in places without money (Believe it or not). It seems like they knew who was homeless and they treated us like that. I caught Broccoli and was very sick. I had to go take a TB Screening Test. I was feeling very sick. Since I had to go to the Doctor for the screening I decided to see the doctor about me felling bad. My fever was so high and by being homeless they let me go home. The Doctor would have kept me but he judged me (I believed this because I was homeless). (Don't Judge Where A Person Comes From; Just Love and Help Them Please). The Doctor told me to go home to the Shelter (I told him where I was living) stay in bed and drink plenty of fluids (Water too.) Gave me some prescriptions and I was able to get them filled at Grady.

My medicine costed $2.00 and someone in the waiting area gave it to me. I told that person God bless you and thank you for being kind. Had to give my medication at the front desk at the Shelter. You only get one cup of juice, coffee or tea to drink at breakfast or dinner time. I had high fever and was very weak. I asked the lady in charge could I stay inside. Showed her my Doctor records (Papers) and my medications. She replied no, no. I put my Pride down called my daughter (Big, big mistake, I was making and made). She came with an attitude saying; why did you come here? On our way to her house she began to tell me how I didn't come to her graduation (that was twenty years ago or more). You see; she never forgave me for not coming (Please pray for her). I was so sick I guess I answered back the wrong way. She said they told me not to pick you up; just leave you there. She said where you want me to bring you because you are not coming with me. I said Mc Donald's in Love Joy. She put me and my clothes out at Mc Donald's. It was about 4pm in the afternoon. I asked the manager there could I stay here until somebody come for me (at this time I didn't know who). I wanted to call the Policeman. I thought at least I would have somewhere to sleep and eat. I have never went to jail before. I called my daughter friend. We became friends as a mother and daughter. She came for me at about 11:30pm that night and brought me to her house.

CHAPTER 16

Doctor of All Doctors

Now The Miracle Is About To Take Place.

I met her girlfriend Ma who became my friend. I lived between her and Ma until my Section 8 came in. The Apartment Manager where they lived said I can have an apartmen. I got a very nice apartment in Fairburn, Georgia and still was smoking cigarettes. I would walk about four blocks down the highway to the Gas Station. I would see this Doctor office over and over again. God gave me favor again. **I heard the Voice of God say, you have Pass the Test of Rejection.** Do you trust me said God. I use to carry all those bags and suitcases around that was pulling me down? I said, yes I trust you Lord. Then God said do you see that Doctor Office at the highway? I replied yes Father. Make an appointment to see the Doctor. God said when you see her tell her that you have Breast Cancer.

I made the appointment with that Doctor. God wanted her and he selected her to see his Glory in me. I Stop smoking and started seeking Jesus even more. I remember in my twenties I use to go to Charity Hospital (TB Clinic in New Orleans) for a knot in my left breast. The knot disappeared (Keep listening). I remember you had to go W16 in Charity hospital to see a Doctor. You would spend a night sleeping in chairs waiting for your name to be called. So I waited with so many other people. Fearful because I just received Christ. Not all the way but did received him. While waiting for my name to be called I began to read the Bible

(1 Peter and 1 John). There were a mixed couple who ask what I was reading. I told them what I was reading and told them about Jesus. They were told that they had aides. I Minister the Word of God and they got

saved (said the Sinners Prayer). But I still had this big knot on my left breast. Then I began to minister to 2 or 3 more people and they got saved too. To God Be The Glory. My name was called and the Doctor said; he think I have Cancer. I said no to the Doctor. It took me months to get an appointment to the Cancer Clinic that he had recommended for me to do. They had so many people that was before me. You see; the Doctors at W16 will just give you news in a way that it was hard to accept(they way they said it without remorse). You really don't want to hear this but need to hear what they had to say. He told me and who to contact to get into the Cancer Clinic. I remember going to the Clinic walking through the doors and hearing Chains. Voices yelling and coldness I can't explain until this day. They took a sample of blood from me and I had to wait another month to hear the results. Could you image what I am going through? All I was during was praying to God day and night. God wanted me to know that he was the Great Healer, Doctor. They decided to take fluid from the knot that was in my left breast. They gave me no pain medication, just the biggest needle I had ever seen. I began to pray and ask God to put the pain in my face. While they was drawing the fluid out my breast; one of the Doctors said; look at her face. I knew God was with me all the way. The Doctors decided to get a Biopsy done. I was put into this room that was so cold. I was undressed on a cold table with a sheet only to cover me. I was waiting for the Pathologist to come in. I had been there waiting so long for the Doctor. I found out later that the Pathologist was in surgery doing a frozen section. I was talking to God and he began to tell me what to tell the Pathologist when she comes in. I knew she was a she because God told me. I saw her when she came into the room. She began to say how sorry she was for taking so long. Then God had me to minister to her. What I said I don't know until this day. For about five to ten minutes God was speaking through me. Then I heard crying. I looked; and it was the Doctor was in a corner crying. She was saying about how much God has done for her. How she forgot about him. Then she came to me to do the Biopsy but the knot was gone. She began to scream and other Doctors came in the room. She told them that I had no knot in my breast. The Doctors told her that they just drawn fluid from it. It's impossible they said and she said no it's not that's Jesus. I left without an Biopsy and Cancer Free in Jesus name. (Luke 18:27) (Matthews 6: 33-34). Now back to Georgia. The Lady

Ma and I began to be good friends. We would help each other with food, money, etc. I told her that I made an appointment and she came with me. When I saw Doctor CF I liked her. She showed love towards her patients (Well I know towards me). Had to give the Nurse information before she came in. I didn't know she was a Holistic Doctor (They Believe in Natural Medication). She began to ask me about what medication that I was taken. I told the Doctor I take No Medication. Then she said you are the one I have been waiting for. God told me to take care of you. Wow!! I didn't know God Loves me so much that he chose someone to take care of me. What's the matter and why no medication. I said God is my Healer and he gives Doctors; Wisdom and Knowledge to tell me what's wrong with my body. Then I take them Spirits to God and he would destroys them (I would call them out in the name of Jesus with Faith to Believe that they had to go). Yes; because I believe he can. God told me to tell you that I have Breast Cancer. She examines me and founded a knot in my Left Breast. We became friends in Christ. She was his friend and I was too. Ma and I went to a Clinic that Doctor CF sent me to for testing. She ordered a Mammon Gram and an Ultra Sound on my Left Breast. TheTech there treated me like I looked. I was kind of dirty looking because my cousin apartment was broken in to. I went with her at her apartment and help clean it up and then it was time for my appointment. I didn't have time to take a shower so I washed under my arms and face. My clothes were not so clean and she looked at that and treated me like I was no body. I told Doctor CF what happen and how theTech treated me. She called the Doctor in charge and told him that I was her Special Patient and if this happen again to any of her Patients of hers' she would stop sending them over there. The Doctor in charge apologizes to me and Doctor CF and had the Tech to apologize to me as well over DF cell phone with speakers on. He said this will never happen again. My Doctor didn't play when it came to her Patients. (Oh God how many more Doctors can you send like Doctor CF who loves and care for your people). So now I have Breast Cancer. She wanted me to call once a week to see her. Waiting for them to call me to do a Biopsy. They finally called me. I was very fearful but not about getting the Biopsy but only of God. Making sure that I represented him in his Love, Peace and Joy that he had given me. Showing them that was not fearful and how I trusted in Gods' Word. I got the results back saying and showing on the Ultra Sound that it was Cancer and it had been there for over 14 years. Doctor CF asked me how long I think it has been there. She said because it is Impossible to have Cancer without it exploring. I told her what I remembered. About 24 years ago a Doctor told me I had Cancer. She started Glorifying God, saying Thank You Jesus.

Dr. CF said; this is going to be Unbelievable to other Doctors.

So The War Begins!

Two Hospitals wanted me.

Emory and Piedmont in Georgia. God sent me to his best in Georgia(I Believe).

I was a Rare Case also a Unbelievable Case. So now all negativity is coming to me. My Mother told me I need to get Chemo and Radiation if needed. My Daughters said nothing and never called me or came to see me. My Aunt went with me to the Cancer Center one time (Thanking God for her). She told my Mother and Daughters that they need to see about me. My Aunt never called or came again I had a daughter who was and still is living in Georgia. But I heard not a word from her. Now Ma and Doctor CF was there for me and most of all ; Jesus. Trying to decide what I was going to do. **I Just Lifted Up the Name of Jesus All the Time. I Read My Word and Began To Live His Word.**

I would go to Doctor CF office dressing for Jesus. You see ; I couldn't go into her office looking like I am Fearful after I told them about Jesus. I told them about his Love, Peace and Joy. So every day I would let God dress me. I would ask God what I should wear today. Should I wear your Love, Joy, Peace, Goodness, Gentleness, Faith, Meekness Temperance or Long Suffering. You see; I wanted them that had no Hope in Living to see how I am living in God with Breast Cancer. I would get in the Zone with God and forget about me and cry out for the Fearful, Hopeless people that I saw at Dr. Cf office and at the Breast Cancer Center. I would see people come to Doctor CF and Pay a Lot of Money for Special Medication to be Put in Their Hearts to Destroy the Cancer they had. I tried to tell them that the Love of God would Heal them (Romans 12: 9-10) (1 John 4: 7) (Roman 13: 10-14). I believe through The Spirit of God I was showing how Powerful God Is. I would not get Chemo or Radiation because I heard through The Grape Vine that this is God's Body not Mines

(1 Corinthians 6: 19-20). I am receiving all kinds of negative phone calls from my family in Christ. There were some people who were on the Prayer Line that God gave to me spoke negative also. One told me ; Pastor Elect we got to die with something. I told her don't call me any more while I am going through this. One of the Evangelist Husband who was not saved spoke to me. He told me a Story about Negativity. I decided to change my phone number and just communicate with the Evangelist, Ma, Doctor CF and Jesus only.

Now dreams of the Devil were kicking in. I would have all kind of dreams at night that cause me to seek God even more. I went to a Holiness Church when I first got saved. Lot of members there died from Cancer. (Just Listen) I saw the Brothers and Sisters I use to go to Church with me; who was dead at a house. They tried to get me to come with them. I said you all are dead. They said just come and see. I fought them through the Spirit of God with his Word. The Trust I have in Gods' Word is just believing in who sent him and in him. Then the next night I saw a Dark Cloud and a little White Sheep inside of this Dark Cloud. The Sheep began to jump. And every time the Sheep jumped the darkness would leave until it all left. Now the Big Boy. I saw a Large Scorpion and a Large Snake. I jumped on the Scorpion back and wounded him but it still was alive. I kept jumping on the Scorpion back until he laid still. The Snake begin to come after me. I began to call on the name of Jesus. He know our calls; whether it's Danger, Hurt, Pain or etc. He heard my cry for help. I woke up as Ma was knocking at the door. She said it's time to go to the Doctor. You see; Ma said the Sinners Prayer with me but was a Babe in Christ. So that means, she was looking at everything I did; everything. She watched how I spoke and how I Praise and Worship God. Ma and I began to walk to the Doctor. Ma would put her Ear Plugs in her Ears to listen to Gospel Music. I would be just sing to God while I was walking. She was walking faster than me. I was just taking my time with God, especially because it was time for me to make a decision with Doctor CF. I didn't want Doctor CF to see me being Fearful and Doubting God. I was just taking my time. **Then I heard Gods' Voice; Don't Move. Don't make another Step. He said look at your Right. When I looked down I saw a Snake with his**

Mouth Open. It was ready to bite me if I had made another step. I begin to call Ma in a low sound voice and she was able to hear me. Then I knew God was with me. She had to be at least ½ block from me with ear plugs in her ears. She said what Mama and I said a Snake waiting to bite me. She came, saw the Snake and said I can jump on his head. No, no; he will bite me and kill me. She said what you are going to do. I said I am going to call on the name of Jesus. I called Jesus and he said to me do you trust me. I replied yes; Father I trust you. Come in the Zone with me. Ma is so amazed she doesn't know what to say or do. I begin to listen to The Voice of God. I closed my eyes and listen to his Voice. He said Heavenly Child slide over to your left until I tell you to begin to walk. I did as God told me and I got to Ma. Jesus told me not to look back at all. I started walking asking Ma where the Snake was. She said he is still there with his mouth open. So amazing; she couldn't believe it or me or Doctor CF (Acts 5:29) (1Corinthians 10:13) (Matthews 10: 28) (Luke 10:19). I begin to tell Doctor CF about the Snake and she said Jesus took me over that Snake. Then Jesus said; **No; I took your Flesh down the street and left your Spirit there**. I didn't understand it then but I understand it now. **You see; a Snake is Sensitive to the Blood that Runs through your Body. God left my Spirit there with the Snake because it had no Power over the Spirit of God and no blood runs through the Spirit of God. (Romans 13:1) (1Corinthians 14:32).** We got home looked the Snake up to see what kind it was. It was a beautiful yellow, white, black and gray in a diamond shape. **It was a Diamond Black Rattle Snake.**

Now you know why I love Jesus so much. The Devil lost again.

I ask God to help me make a decision where to go. Emory was so far but I would pay Mr. Jon to bring me there and back.

We would go to Doctor CF office and would have to wait for a long time (Dr. CF would give her Patients a lot of time and talk to them until they would understand her with the Love of God; I believed This). We would be so thirsty and there were nothing to drink but water. I told Ma if I was working at Doctor CF office I would buy drinks and water and give them to her patients for free.(Please Remember This).

Now it's time to go to Piedmont Hospital in Fayetteville. Ma and I went there and we were so thirsty. Got in the room and the Doctors' Nurse offer us something to drink, she said I have sodas and water. I looked at

Ma and said this is the place God wants me to have my operation. Ma said how do you know that. Ma Remember what I said at Doctor CF office about sodas and water.

Now Dr. SK ; I liked her too. She begins to tell me I had Cancer and they wanted to do a fast surgery on me. It has been there too long. They were going to send my sample to New York City so they can examine it. I replied, yes it's okay. Only one week later its surgery time. I had no one but Jesus in the Spirit and Ma in the Flesh. So three days before surgery my doctor asked who will be staying with me. Ma said; I will stay with her. So Fear is trying to kick in. I wasn't letting it do so. Ma and I prayed together all night. Two days before surgery; Jesus came to me and spoke to me. Saying the Angels will be there. They will light up the Operation Room and I will do the Surgery on you. I need you to call your Doctor and tell her what I said. Jesus said tell her he will do the operation, let him guide her hands. Don't move them other than when he moves them. So I called Dr. SK and told her what God said. Dr. SK would call me Sunshine; I don't know why but that was my name to her. I called her, left a message and she called me back so fast. What's the matter Sunshine. I said I need to tell you what God said. So I told her what God said. She replied; I hear you but I know what to do. I said did you hear what God said again. He also said that the Angels was going to be in the operation too. Please follow his instructions for me and you. Dr. SK pauses and said nothing. I said; agree to what God said or I will not have the operation. (You see; I was a special case that maybe they never had before). They couldn't believe this Cancer was in me over fourteen years or more. (I say twenty or more). Well they wanted to see this Miracle. So after a minute or two then Dr. SK said Yes and gave me Her Word. I will see you on Friday and Thank you. If you talking about Fear; I had it. First; I had to go to the Cancer Breast Clinic and get a piece of Iron put inside the Left Breast and that too was a Surgery. Then being escorted by a van to the Cancer Center that was an ½ block away. That surgery took about an hour or more to put that Iron in. Dr. SK came to encourage me (that's how she was; God sent Doctor like Dr CF was too. That's what I loved about her and Doctor CF they let you know they care. Dr. SK is a great asset to Pediment Cancer Center.

Now they are rolling me into the operation room. I could hear the operation team talk about how much light that was in the room. I knew then God is Faithful Evermore. The Angels were present. The Power of their Presences put me to see. The Anesthesiologist Doctor came in and said don't go to sleep. I have to put you to sleep to monitor you. I remember saying Doctor it's too late. The Angels are already here. I could hear them say wake her up she is gone to sleep. Ma said the surgery took about (3) three hours or little more. All I could remember waking up seeing Ma than Dr. SK saying everything came out alright. I was in the recovery room and I heard a Nurse say she just came out the Operation Room and she is woke. Then I told the Nurse when she came in to do my vital signs; I was ready to go home because God delivered me. The Nurse said you can't go home. I ask her to call Dr. SK for me and tell her I desires to go home. Dr. SK said I heard what you said; if she wants to go home let her go (30 minutes after the Surgery). Dr. SK gave me pain medication and I went home. Dr. SK knew that God did the Surgery. I took one (1) pain pill. I didn't believe I had the surgery. The next day I called Dr. SK at her home and asked her about the surgery because I felt no pain. I was moving greatly around the house. God gave me Favor with the Doctors he chose for me. I was able to call them at their homes. They gave me their cell phone numbers (Dr. CF and Dr. SK). I ask her did I have Surgery and did she take it out. She replied; that she not only took that knot out but a little bit more. Dr. SK said Sunshine I never met anyone like you and I said the same thing to her.

Going back to Doctor CF after the surgery that took place a week ago. She was saying Thank You Jesus when I told her what happen. Checkup time came with one of my favorite Doctors Dr. SK (Doctor CF is a favorite too). Talking about Dr. SK she begin to look at the cut and was so proud of how it looked. She suggest for me to get some Vitamin E Oil to rub on the cut. I told her God did this and it will heal. She said please I have an image to up hold. I said I have God to up hold. She looked at me and laughed. She couldn't believe that I was as well as I was in a week after surgery. I told her that God Won Again in my life. I would tell Dr. SK about some Testimonies that God done in my life especially; healing. He has **No Respect of Person**; meaning; he don't care who you are in the world, only who you are in him. And he will do the same thing for you if you believe in who sent him and in him. I would tell Testimonies about my life not only to Adults but to children too. To anyone who had an ear to hear (Romans 2: 11-13).

I could remember people telling me how they did what I said in my testimonies and it worked for them. One night my granddaughter Ms. BJ was on the Prayer Line. I begin to testify how God saved my life from Mr. O. How I heard the Voice of God saying you are asking the wrong one not to kill you. And how I began to ask God to help me (Matthews 10:28). So I was telling the Prayer Line about my granddaughter Ms. BJ and what she called and told me what happen to her. Now Ms. BJ and Mr. BL my granddaughter and grandson use to live with me. Through the Grace of God I raised them in the Life of Jesus Christ. They know that God is real for their selves. I lived the life of someone seeking God. Living the life of the Scriptures in the Bible (Proverbs 22:6). Ms. BJ called and said she almost died. This took place (2) two days after the testimony on the Prayer Line. Ms. BJ said she was by Grandma J house and swallowed a nose ring. I was turning colors and couldn't catch my breath. I was trying to call for help but at first no one heard me. Grandma J, my Mother and everybody that was in the house was trying to help me get the nose ring out my throat. They was hitting me in my back and squeezing my stomach as I was trying to yell and was crying. Then I thought about what you said Grandma Pastor about what God did for you when Mr. O was trying to kill you. Ms. BJ said to herself; if God saved your life Grandma Pastor he could save my life too. So I started calling on Jesus and the nose ring jumped out my throat. I Thank You Grandma Pastor for letting me know about the Power of Jesus.

Now Mr. BL my grandson was about (3) three years old. Ms. BJ was sleep; Mr. BL and I was watching television. Mr. BL begins to Scream and Cry in Fear. I said Mr. BL what's wrong and he said I see a Angel on the dresser. How do you know it's an Angel? He said he has Wings and they are moving. He's in all white and I am Afraid. I said what is he doing to you and he said nothing just looking at me. Mr. BL said Grandma Pastor I am scared. I said do you believe in Jesus and his Power. He said; yes Grandma Pastor but I am Afraid. Then I told Mr. BL to say in the name of Jesus I command (I am telling you) you to leave. I cover myself with the Blood of Jesus. Now I told him if it's an Angel of Jesus, he will stay. But if it's the Angel of the Devil he has to leave because of the Blood of Jesus. So the next night Mr. BL, Ms. B J and I were watching television. I ask Mr. BL do he still see the Angel. He said Yes; Grandma Pastor. Where is he and what is he doing? Mr. BL said he's just looking at me and flapping his wings. I said Mr. BL you are not scared and he said; no. I ask him why and he said because I said in the name of Jesus I command you to leave.

I pleaded the Blood of Jesus and he's still here. Mr. BL said Grandmother Pastor he belongs to God and I am not afraid any more. Then my mouth went open. Ms. B J ; just being Ms.

B J said Grandma Pastor; why you act like you are so surprised? She said; you always ask the Angels to come into this house to protect us. I believe that the Angels are in this house and he saw them.

Tell your children and other children about Jesus. His Word and His Power. Children are just smaller than us but have the same beliefs and understanding as we do.

About two years after Mr. BL and Ms. BJ were returned to their parents. Ms. BJ came to visit me. A Guy down the street from me is a Diabetic and took a lot of insulin. He was shaking so bad. I cooked and called him over to get a hot meal. You see; I use to be a Diabetic but overcame that Spirit through the Grace of God. Once you have overcome a Spirit; you can cast it out someone else. Because those Spirits know who you are (Matthews 7:5). So I begin to hold his hands and Pray for him. Commanding that those Spirits to be still in the name of Jesus. To stop making him shake uncontrollable (he said he don't believe in Jesus). The Diabetic man has to believe that Jesus can do this. So I ask him do you believe that Jesus can do this. (what he was taught about Jesus was wrong). So he completely stops shaking and gave his life to Jesus. Now Ms. BJ mouth open wide. As she begin to say; **Grandma Pastor I know there is a God and I Forgot About His Power**. But I now believe in Jesus again. After I saw this man stop shaking. Please teach your Children, Grand Children and other Children about Jesus. Let them see the Power of God in you. You would really began to see how he would use you in their lives (Matthews 5:16) (Luke 10:20).

The test results of the Cancer came back they called me in to talk. They sent a copy to Doctor CF to see it. When I got there they told me they sent my specimens to New York City and it came back No Cancer. My God got his Glory. He let the scientist that think they are God; that there is only one true God. I had two Biopsy that said it was Cancer. Had test ran over and over; that said it was Cancer. Doctor CF said it was Cancer but they couldn't say it was because it was to Powerful for their Minds. Jesus told me it was Cancer and I believed him. You had it so long it was unbelievable Dr. CF said. They tried at the Cancer Clinic to get me to take Cancer Pills. They said that the Cancer might not come back. I said Doctor; if I didn't have Cancer why would I take pills that cause Blood Clots. They said 80% of patients don't blood clots that kill. I told them that Jesus Healed me. If I take these pills I am saying I don't believe Jesus Healed me. The answer was NO and is still NO. They still until this day they are still trying to persuade me to take Cancer Pills. The Doctor that gives you these pills told his Nurse don't ask me no more about the pills. Because people like her is not going to take them (Those people believe in a Higher Power). Thanking God for him (the Doctor) realizing that there are people who Love, Believe and Trust Jesus. **I took no Chemo or Radiation or Pills just the Love, Peace and Joy of God**. I still get my Mammograms and Ultra Sounds every (6) six months at the Cancer Center and I am Cancer Free.

All Glory, All Honor and All Power to God.

God Won Again.

God let the Doctors, and Scientist know that he is the Doctor of all Doctors.

CHAPTER 17

Believing in What You Pray For

I still had a thorn in my side. I ask God every day to take it away (2 Corinthians 12: 7-9). Don't feel bad when God heals you and you make another mistake against the Law of Christ. Jesus says **My Grace is Sufficient for Thee: for My Strength is made perfect in Weakness.** So next time in your weakness give it all to Jesus. You see; the Devil will never give up on trying to kill us or to have us to serve him (Mark 8: 35-37). In this Scripture I like it because he taught me not to exchange God for no one or anything. **What shall a man give in exchange for his Soul? (Matthews 4:1-11) (Luke 4: 1-13). I like the Scripture in Luke 4:13 that says; and when the Devil had ended all the temptations, he departed from him for a Season. For a Season was Powerful to me.** Letting me know that when; If We Trust God with Our Whole Heart, Mind and Soul We Can Defeat The Devil, The World and Our Flesh. Satan (Devil) rests for a while and tries again. Well this is what he does in my life.

After the Cancer Victory, I don't know how but daughter called Ma to tell me about my daughters' baby that was on the D.I. List (Dying List). My daughter had to a C-Section because her baby stopped breathing. After her C-Section; I was told that the baby bowls (Waste materials) was coming out her mouth. They rush her to Children Hospital preparing her for Surgery. They were waiting for a Special Surgeon to come. At this time; I called my Daughter and her Husband and ask them if they would like to give God their lives and Pray for their baby. Ma and I was praying for the baby since we got the call. So I told them that God said she was going to be alright. Then I told them why not give God your life. Then the phone hangs up. I am thinking I disconnected them but they disconnected me because I told them about Jesus. I called back and Jo said don't tell me that stupid stuff. Now image her daughter is fighting for her life. So Ma and I begin to pray harder. I am giving God the Promises he gave my Father Abraham back in (Genesis 28:14) (Genesis 22:18) (Acts 3:25) (Isaiah 6:19) (John 14:14) (John 16:24) (John 15:16). I ask God to forgive them and the baby was my seed. Ma touched and agreed with me. I ask God send one of his Doctors with his Wisdom and knowledge to my granddaughter. Let them not put her bowls to her side and let her bowls move normally. I heard a Voice say if you want your granddaughter to live, then the sickness will come on you. I said; okay but please give her a chance to live. God to grow and learn of you. Then within two hours later the phone rang. It was my Granddaughters' Mother (my daughter of the world) that said they let her go to the Hospital after just having a C-Section. She said when she got there the Doctor had arrived. He examine her baby and gave her a rectum enema (perhaps 2 or 3). Then her bowls begin move downwards. She didn't need that surgery. I believe when I asked God to send one of his Doctors with his wisdom and knowledge he did just that. **God will do what you ask him. If you just believe in him and who sent him. He can do this for you too.**

Ma and I was rejoicing so much. About thirty minutes later I went to the bathroom and felt something was falling between my legs in my Vagina. I let Ma look at it and she began to scream. She said it's a big mass (meaning something down there is very big). I didn't have much pain (I can take a lot of pain for what I have been through). Went to Doctor CF and she said it's a Prolapse (Meaning my bowls intestine and bladder had dropped and I need Surgery). Went to the Specialist Doctor that told me I needed an operation. I needed a mass put down there. Well I knew what it was but didn't want it because my Body belongs to God (God Didn't Tell Me to Get an Operation)

(1 Corinthians 6: 19-20). I prayed to God and I had no pain and never got the operation until this day. I have lived my life and so if it was to take my life for my granddaughter life; then I did. To take her sickness from her to me; well I did that. I now live with it and it's been about three years now. I don't know if it's because her Parents wouldn't acknowledge Gods' Power or what. I believed no one Sinned (John 9: 3). They did say thanks

for praying for their baby and prays works. It's hard for me to go to the bathroom but I just call on the name of Jesus and go. **God is Faithful. Please give him a chance to prove to you how much he wants to Love you**. The Devil wasn't satisfied because he wants me and he can't have me.

After the healing of my granddaughter I moved back to New Orleans. Everything was looking up for me.

I had to have a Colonoscopy because my Doctor in New Orleans wanted it done. She knew about the Prolapse and didn't want me to get Cancer. I had to see this Miracle Baby, My Seed that God made a Miracle.

I befriended my family again and they destroyed me again. I made an appointment to have a Colonoscopy done. The Doctor told me it will take about fifteen to twenty minutes than recovery for about thrity minutes. Now I wasn't Fearful but just Nerves. I ask my Brother WA who got saved on the Prayer Line to come with me. God allowed him to come with me. Earlier that month I went with him to have his Colonoscopy done. We were out in forty minutes and was finish with everything. So the week before the surgery. **I begin to Pray and Hang All Kinds of Healing Scriptures in My House. (Meaning what I thought through Gods' Word meant Healing. I put them on the mirrors, walls, refrigerator and everywhere.** I would look at them all the time. Didn't talk to negative people at all. Just continue praying and believing in God. Now I am ready, prayed up and talking to God. I ask God to let the Angels be in the room with me and for him to do the operation. Getting rolled in the operation room I met a Gay guy who was in the operation room. There were another lady there but she didn't talk as much as XL (He was the Gay Guy). When I heard and saw the movement of XL I begin to Judge him. I said; look how the Devil did this. He gave me one of his. Then I began to talk to God. God wouldn't answer me. The Holy Spirit told me God was mad with me for making such a judgment. While XL was talking to the lady, I began to repent to God, saying how sorry I was to make such a judgment on your people. I promise God I would never do that again. So I kept praying and talking to God. Father give me another chance to prove to you that I want do this anymore. So as XL began to talk to me kind, I responded kind (he was the most kind and soft speaking person I ever met in the operation room). He would make you feel like it's okay and will be okay. Then I ask God saying; God I ask you to have the Angels present for me. God said;

what did you say? I said Father please help me. Where are the Angels? Turn on your right side; I heard the lady that was helping him say this to me? Did you see what I saw said XL? The lady said I was going to ask you what that was? XL said that's Angels. They have Angels in this room. Then I said to XL can you come here and say what you said. He said I don't know who you are but there are Angels in this room. I said I know XL because I ask God to send them. I asked for them to be here. **Then XL begins to be Speechless and said I have Chills all over me. You see; He saw the Power of God just as He was (Gay). Never make Judgment on What and Who God Created.** Then the Doctor came in, I could hear XL telling him about the Angels. My surgery took about one hour and fifteen minutes long. The Doctor told me that there were 50 cents pieces of mass and 25 cents pieces of mass that he moved. We normally don't remove those big masses he said. But I didn't know why I just continue moving them until all was gone. My brother WA was so serious he said; he kept asking the Nurses what's going on with my sister. He said; she has been in there for a long time now. They finally put me in the recovery room. I woke up ten minutes later and saw my brother and the Doctor talking.

I listen to the Doctors' report and then ask him to call XL for me. I wanted XL to tell my brother who was in the operation room. XL did just that and said I do believe in God now.

I testify to this because I wanted you to know as long as You Live for Jesus, Walking Like Him, Believing in His Word and Trusting Him; Jesus will Protect You. The Devil will leave but will come back and back. Until you have become an Overcomer of All Things, Not Some But All. As long as you stay with Jesus you will become an Overcomer of All Things. You see; I have nothing to complaint about. When you pray for something; be ready to receive what you prayed for. My life has been a life to tell someone else. **Don't Think It Strange; Just Stay With The One Who You Think Is Strange (JESUS).**

WHY THE TITLE IS

The Love That Once Healed Me Is The Same Love That Destroys Me.

When I was born My Mother gave Me
enough Love to Survive and then Destroyed Me.
Then I got Married to Mr. X and he
Healed me from Abuse and then Destroyed Me with Abuse.
My Mother-in-Law Loved Me like
Mothers' should and Healed Me from
Not being Motherly Loved then Destroyed Me with
Teaching me to live with Controlling Love
My Three Daughters Healed Me
With their Joy of Birth and then Destroyed Me with their Separation
Mr. O. Healed Me with Time and
Fake Words that No One Told me
Before; Then Destroyed Me by
Beating Me Half To Death.

THE RESULTS

Then one day I met Jesus. I found out after being with Jesus that he has a Love that Heals you and will never Hurt you. All them that Healed Me with Fake Love and Destroyed Me with the Enemy Love; Can't Do It Again. Gods' Love keeps on Healing Me Over and Over.

Try Him and See How He Will Keep Healing You with His Love. If you don't know Jesus but wants this Special Healing of Love; Then Repeat This. You will be Giving God your Life. As God has given this Prayer to me I give it to you. If You Say This Prayer, You Will Never Be The Same:

NOW BEFORE YOU SAY THIS PRAYER. I WOULD LIKE YOU TO SING THIS SONG TO YOURSELF. GOD GAVE THIS TO ME TO LET ME KNOW I CAN'T STOP WITHOUT HIM.

IF I COULD-----IF I COULD--
I SURELY WOULD—
I SURLEY WOULD----
IF I COULD-STOP (NAME IT)
(SINNING) IF I COULD--STOP--
I SURLEY WOULD---
I SURLEY WOULD---
BUT OH GOD—OH MY LORD--
I NEED YOU LORD---
I NEED YOU LORD--
CAUSE--IF I COULD-STOP--(NAME IT) (REPEAT THIS)
I SURLEY WOULD-I SURLEY WOULD. (REPEAT) OH MY GOD--I NEED YOU LORD---

YOU CAN'T STOP. BUT GOD CAN STOP YOU FROM SINNING. (GO FOR IT)

SINNERS PRAYER

I Confess With My Mouth and Believe In My Heart That Jesus Is The Only Begotten Son Of God. He Died And Rose And Is Sited At The Right Hand Of The Father. And To His Kingdom There No End. I Renounce Satan (Devil) And His Adversaries. That They Can No Longer Be Lord Over My Mind, Heart Or Soul Anymore In Jesus Name. I Ask You Jesus To Come Into My Heart, Mind And Soul And Be My Lord And Savior In Jesus Name Amen (Romans 10:9).

I Pray These Testimonies Will Help You To Be Victorious In Jesus.

TO THE AUTHOR AND READERS

————————•——————————

PROPHETESS
COLOUMBUS, GEORGIA

THIS BOOK IS AN AWESOME BOOK. AS I BEGIN TO READ THIS BOOK; IT BROUGHT HEALING TO MY MIND AND SOUL. I COULD RELATE TO BEING REJECTED. THIS BOOK OPENS MY EYES AND ENLIGHTENS ME ABOUT GODS' GRACE, MERCY AND HIS LONG SUFFERING TOWARDS US. HIS POWER TO HEAL AND TO SET THE CAPTIVES FREE.

A 12 YEAR OLD GIRL FROM NEW ORLEANS, LOUISIANA.

THIS IS AN EYE OPENING FOR A LOT OF PEOPLE.
I KNOW NOW THAT GOD IS REAL. HOW MUCH HE LOVES US.
I JUST CALL THE BOOK AN EYE OPENER.

THE UNKNOWN PROPHET
GODS' KINGDOM

THIS BOOK IS AN EYE OPENER FOR ME. IT REMINDED ME ABOUT THE LOVE GOD HAD AND STILL HAVE FOR ME. IT REMINDED ME HOW AMAZING GOD IS; IF YOU BELIEVE IN HIM AND WHO SENT HIM. IT REMINDED ME IF GOD DID IT THEN; HE CAN DO IT AGAIN. JESUS CHRIST IS THE SAME YESTERDAY AND TODAY AND FOREVER (HEBREWS 13:8).

Printed in the United States
By Bookmasters